About The Author

Hi, My name is Dai'Jon Pryor. I will be eleven years old on May 12th, 2019. I am currently in the Fifth grade! I was born in 2008 on Mother's Day in the state of California. I began writing when I was seven years old and drawing at the age of three years old. My hobbies are drawing, writing, reading, acting, creative inventing, exercising, Gymnastics, Martial Arts, playing Basketball, studying computer's, and playing the Guitar, Violin, Flute, Harmonica, Saxophone, Piano, Trombone, and Drums. When I grow up, I want to become an Artist, Architect, Forensic Artist, Actor, Movie Director, Inventor, Business Investor, Realtor, Personal Fitness Trainer, Inspiring Advocate Speaker for the Youth, and continue on being a successful Author and Illustrator. I am very excited about publishing my Children's Book called, Look Inside. I'm really proud of my little sister Kah'Lonee' Pryor accomplishment on publishing her Recipe Book called, Kah'Lonee' Sunny Days Recipes. I am currently working on my Comic Book to be published by the year of 2020. My Parents, my little Sister, my Uncles, and Grand Parents are my supporter's and motivator's. I love my Parents, I love my Grand Parents, I love my Family, I love my little Sister and the rest of my Sibling's! I enjoy being a kid, making people laugh and meeting new friends. In the past, I have attended Martial Arts, Male Commercial Modeling, Acting Classes, Tumbling and Gymnastics, and played Flag Football and Baseball. I've been awarded plenty of Trophies, Certificates, and Rewards, but my major accomplishment was being the fastest reader in my third grade class; reading, spelling, and typing at a sixth grade level. With this all being shared, hopefully you'll enjoy my Coloring Book, think outside of the box, have fun being a kid, learn more and always believe in yourself. I personally, want to give praise to God for all of my blessing's, talent's, gift's and strength. Next, I want to give much appreciation to my Mother who is loving, caring, beautiful, strong, educated, and the best Mother ever! Lastly, I'll like to dedicate this book to my Father!

About The Book:

DP Arts Coloring Book was designed, illustrated and published to share stories through my creative drawing's! Drawing and coloring are two of the best ways to relax your mind, brainstorm, expand your thoughts, be creative, and enjoy seeing a variety of Artwork. I like to believe each piece of Art has multiple meaning's, but they can only be defined through the Artist and colors used.

DP Arts
Coloring Book

DP Arts
Coloring Book

Dai'Jon Pryor

Copyright © 2018 by Dai'Jon Pryor.

ISBN:	Softcover	978-1-9845-6069-8
	eBook	978-1-9845-6068-1

All rights reserved. No part of this book may be reproduced or transmitted in any form or by any means, electronic or mechanical, including photocopying, recording, or by any information storage and retrieval system, without permission in writing from the copyright owner.

The views expressed in this work are solely those of the author and do not necessarily reflect the views of the publisher, and the publisher hereby disclaims any responsibility for them.

Any people depicted in stock imagery provided by Getty Images are models, and such images are being used for illustrative purposes only.
Certain stock imagery © Getty Images.

Print information available on the last page.

Rev. date: 10/22/2018

To order additional copies of this book, contact:
Xlibris
1-888-795-4274
www.Xlibris.com
Orders@Xlibris.com
783235

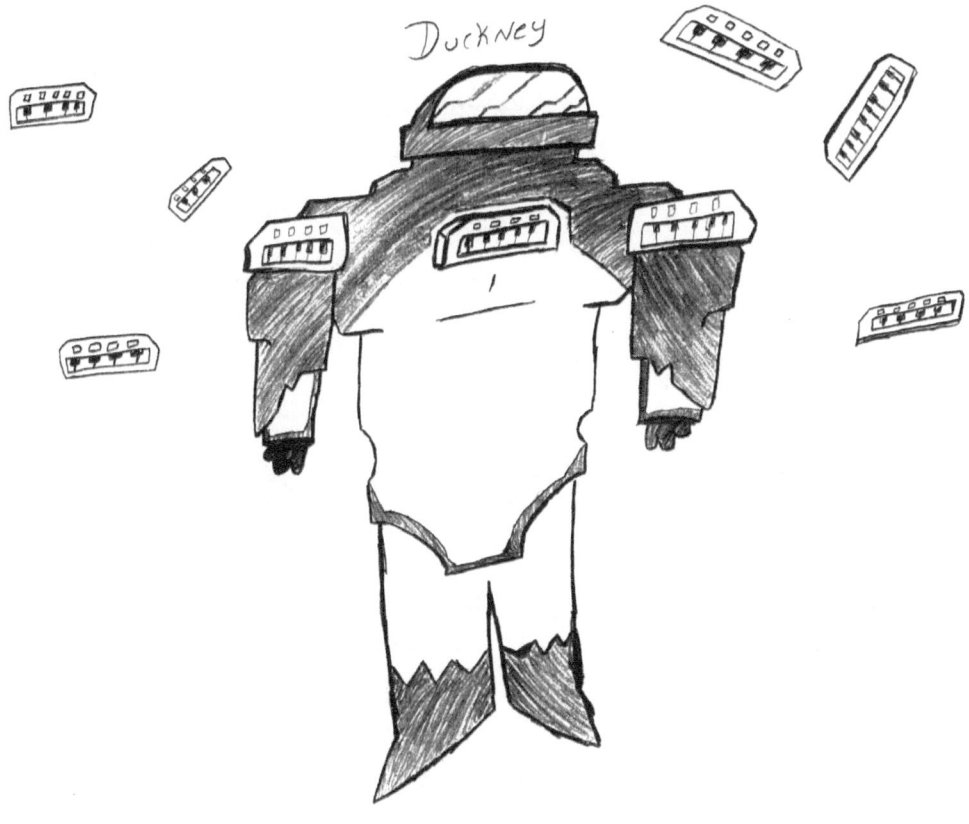

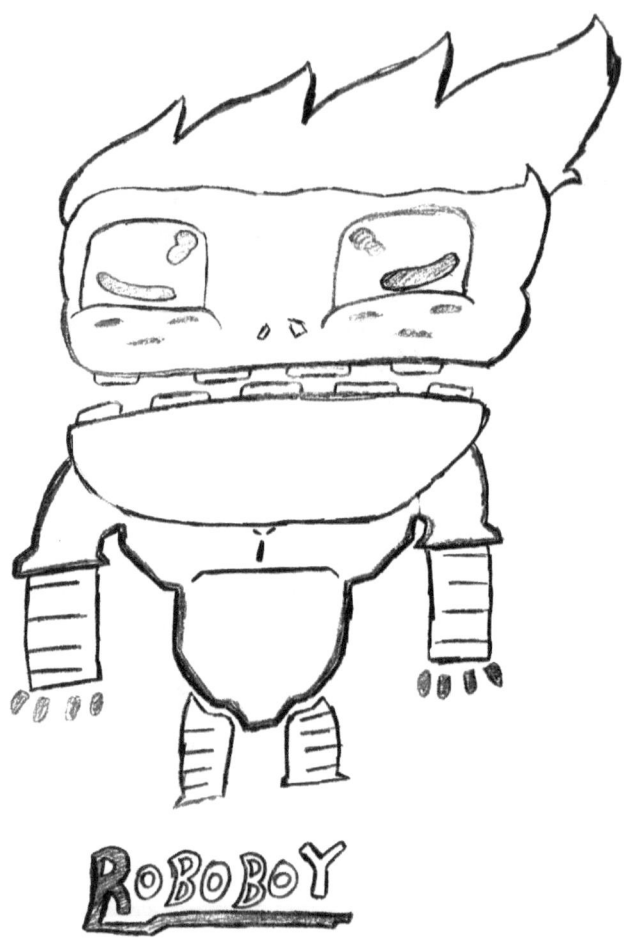

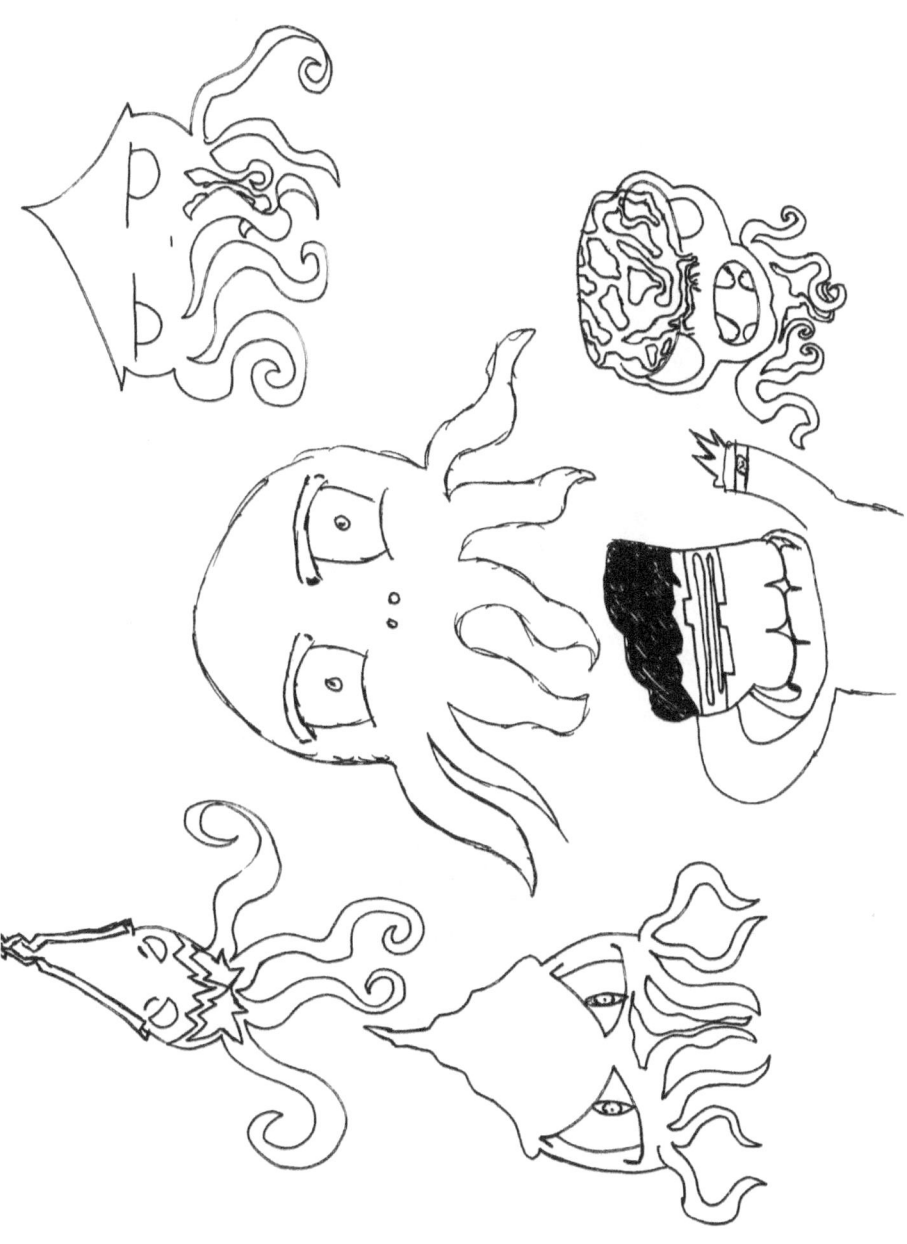

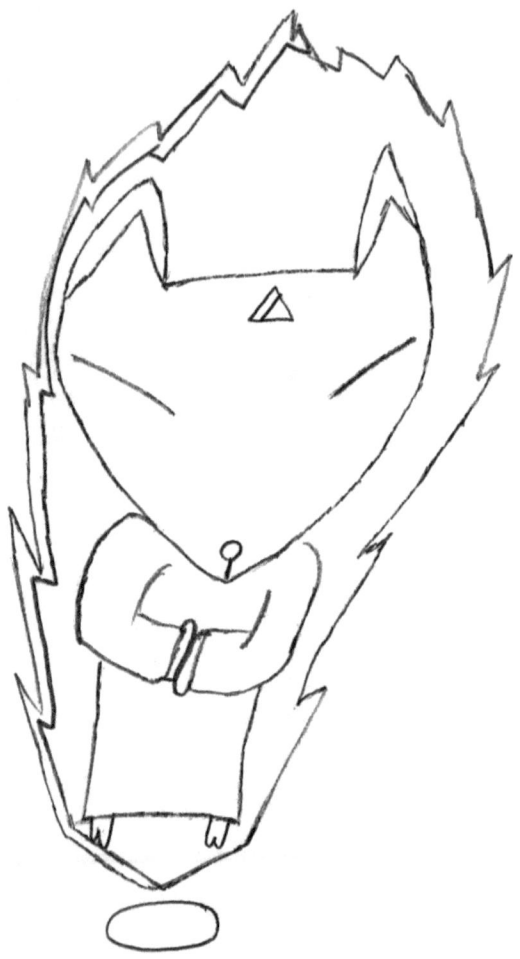

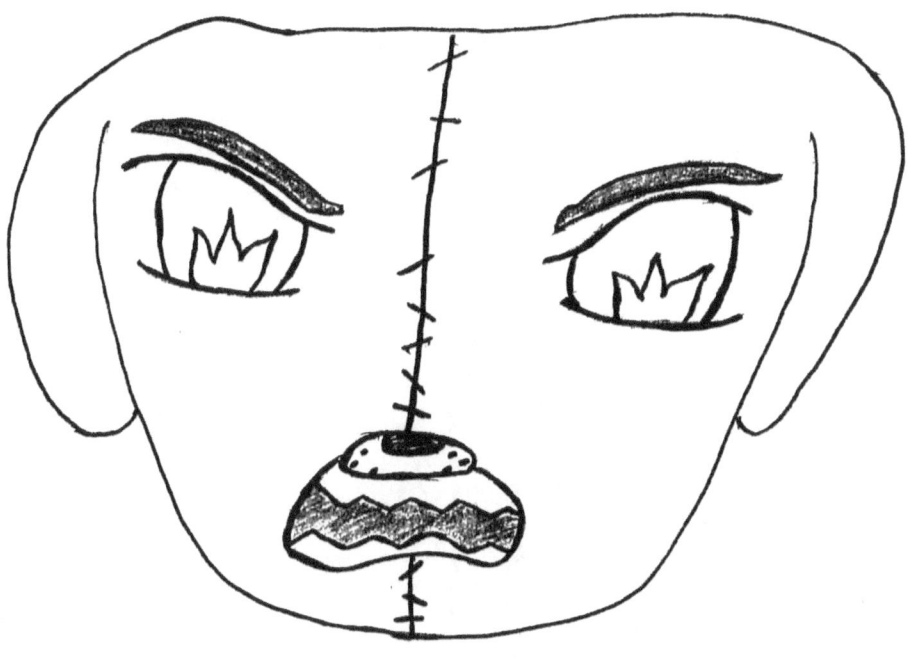

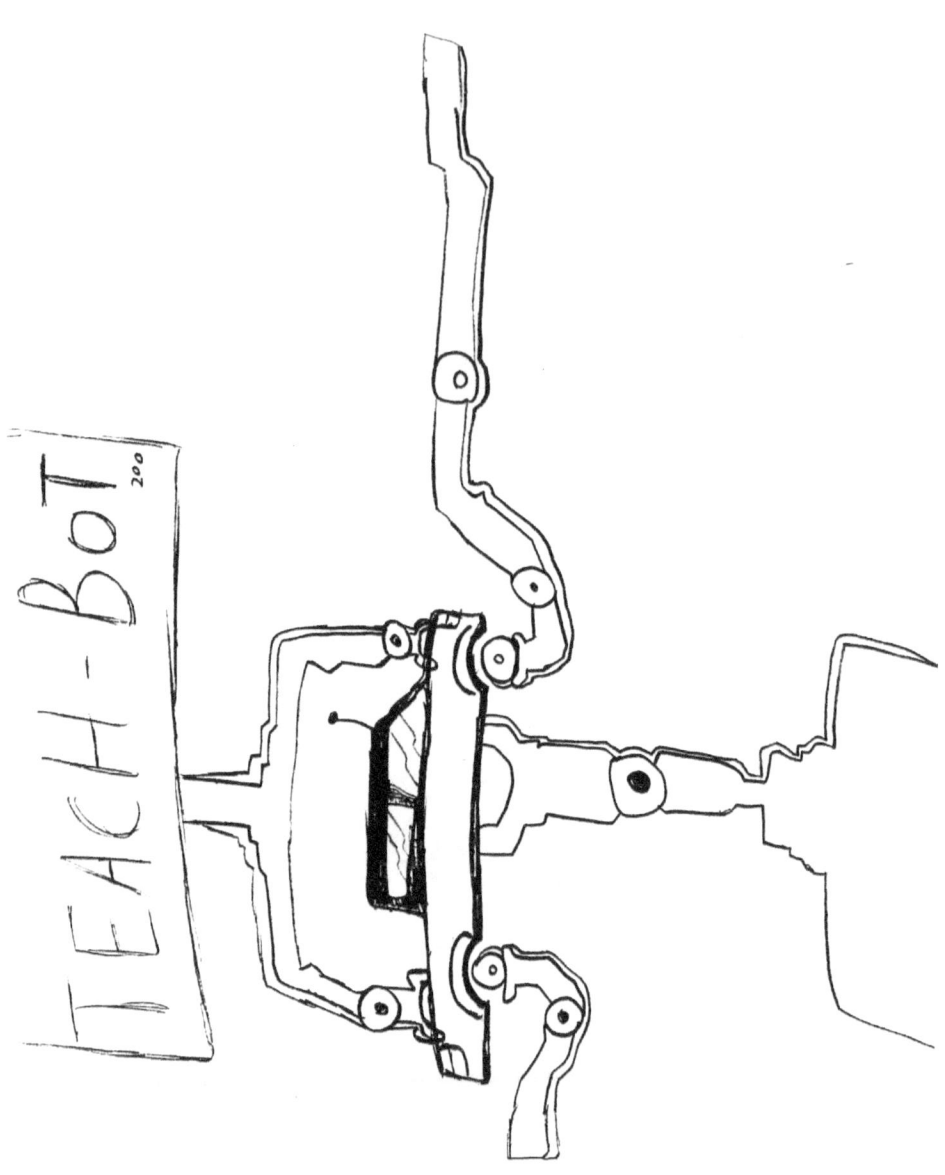

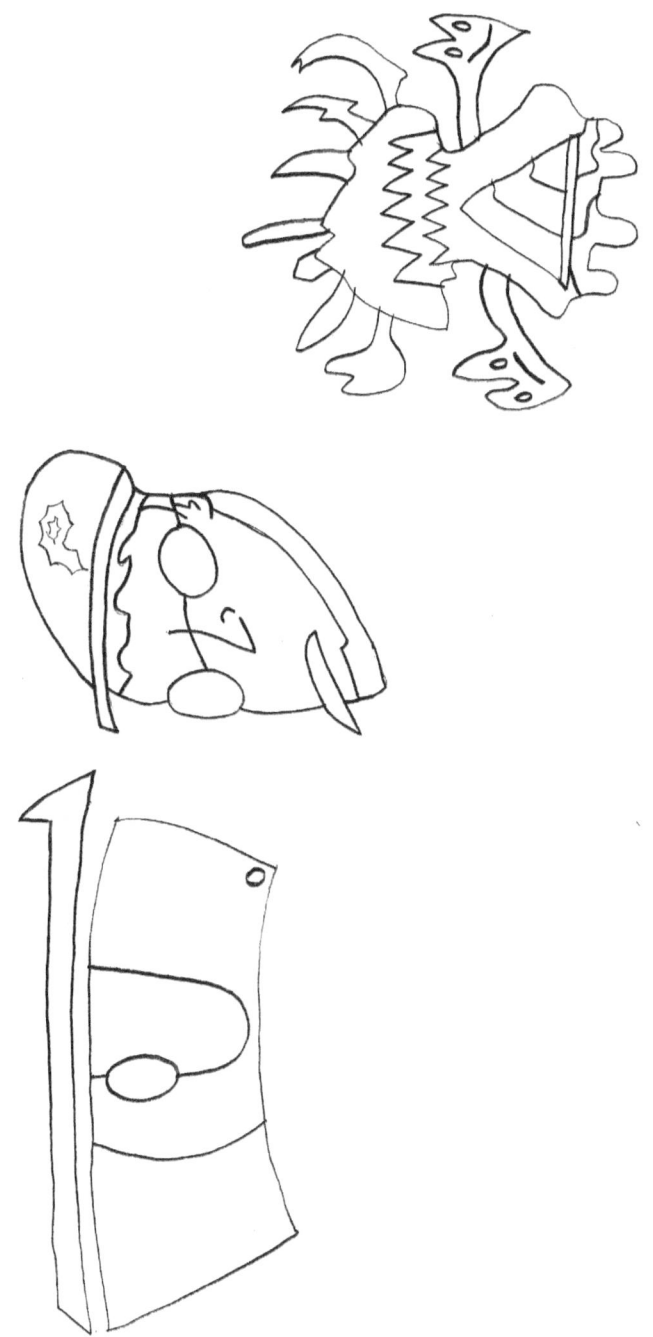

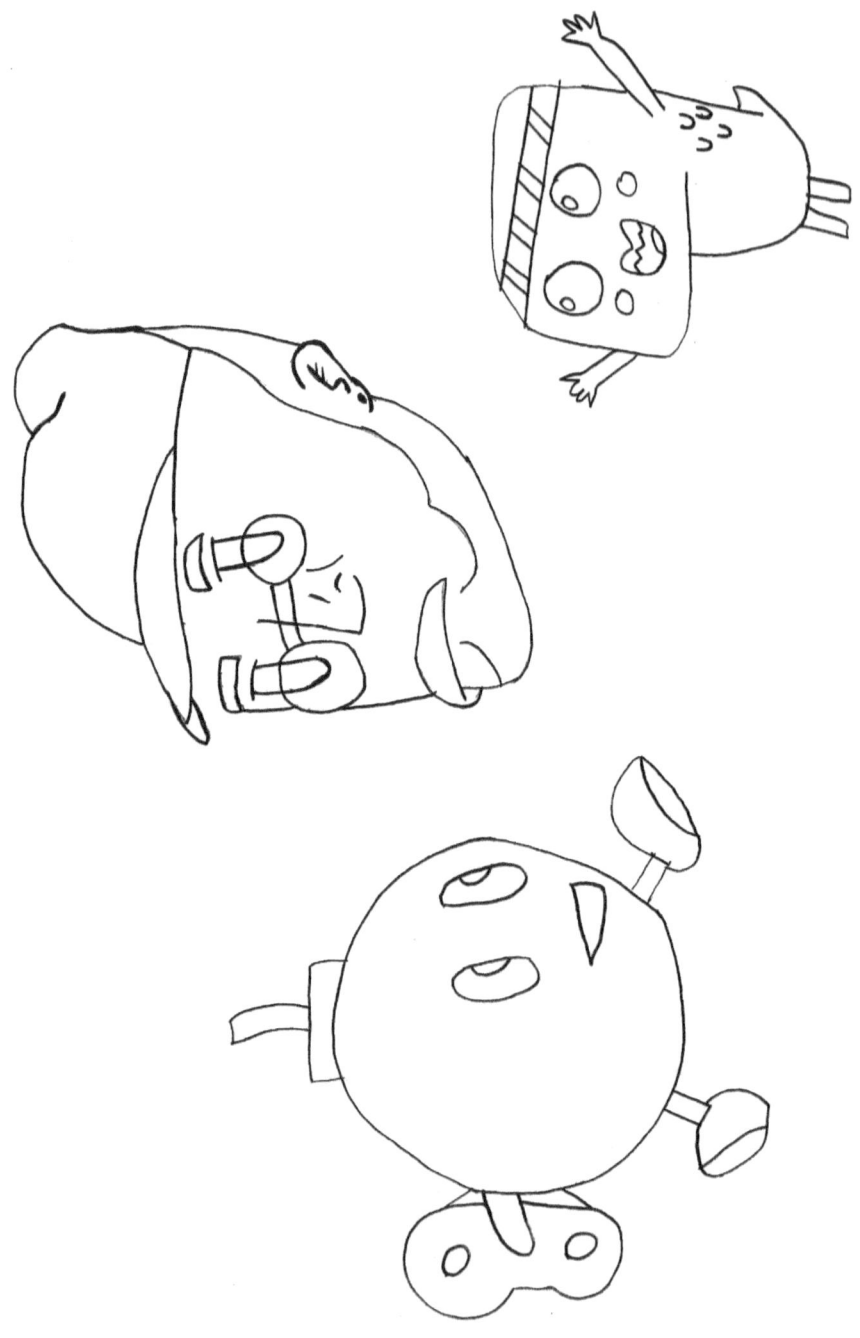

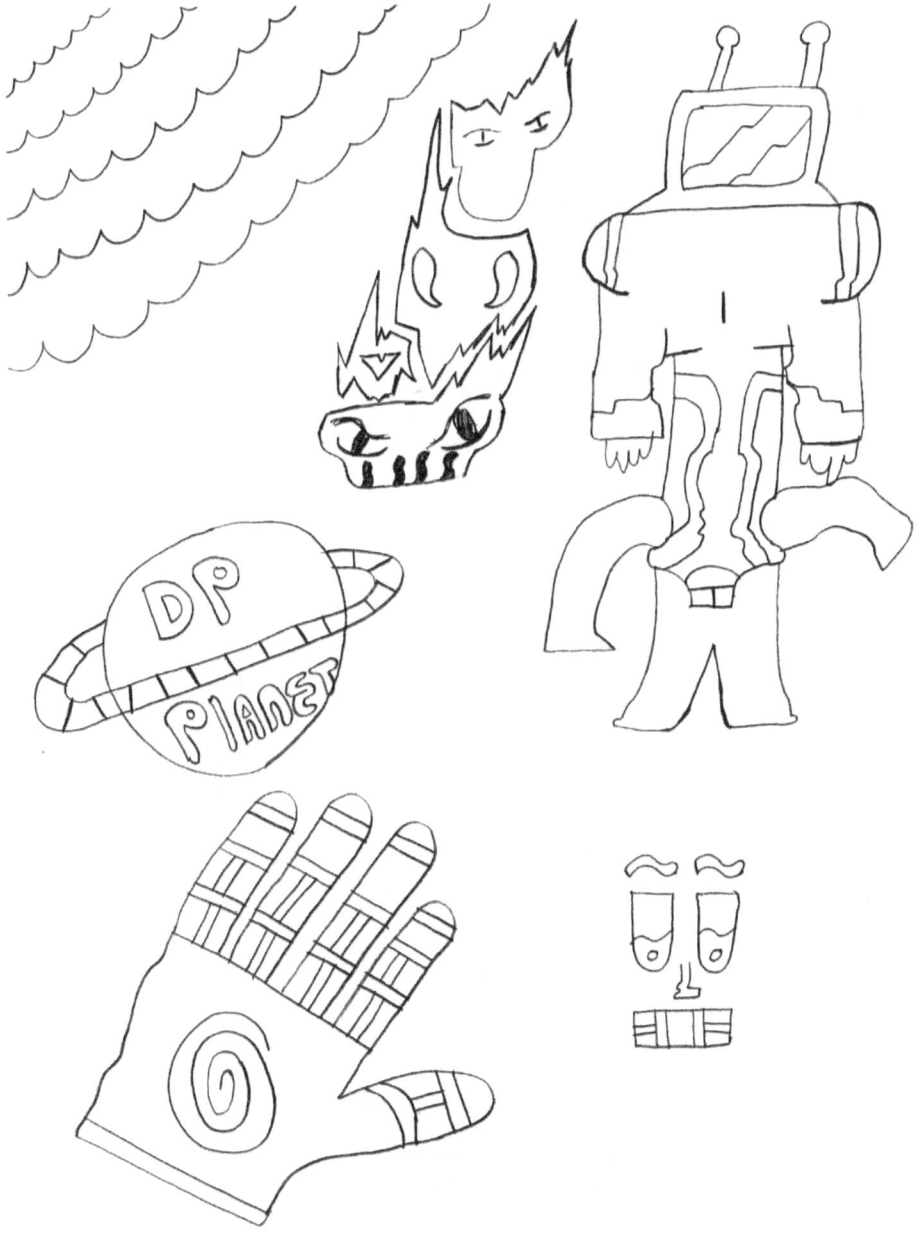

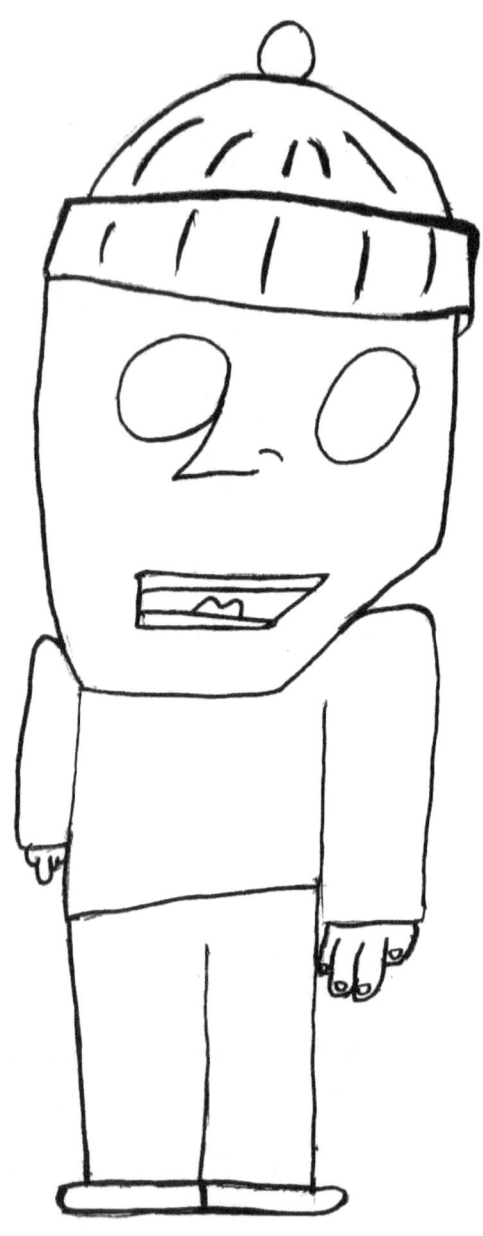

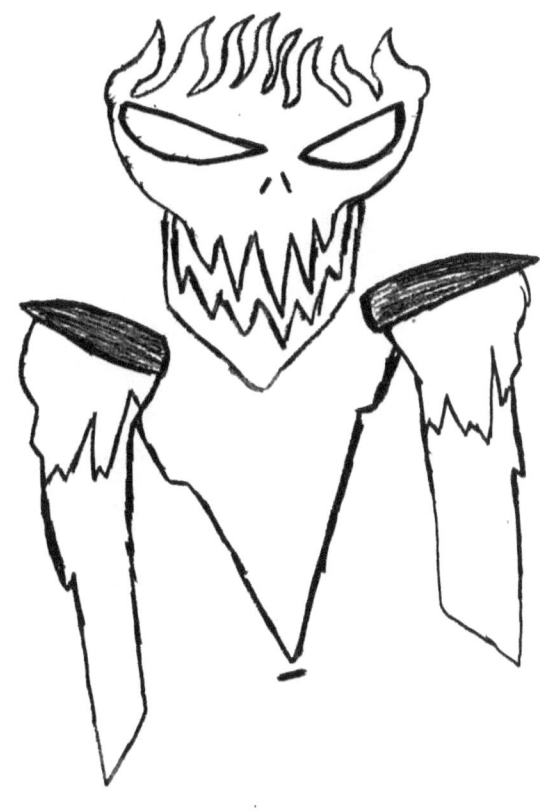
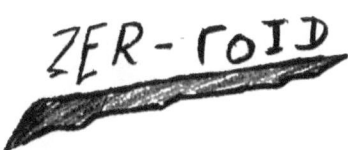

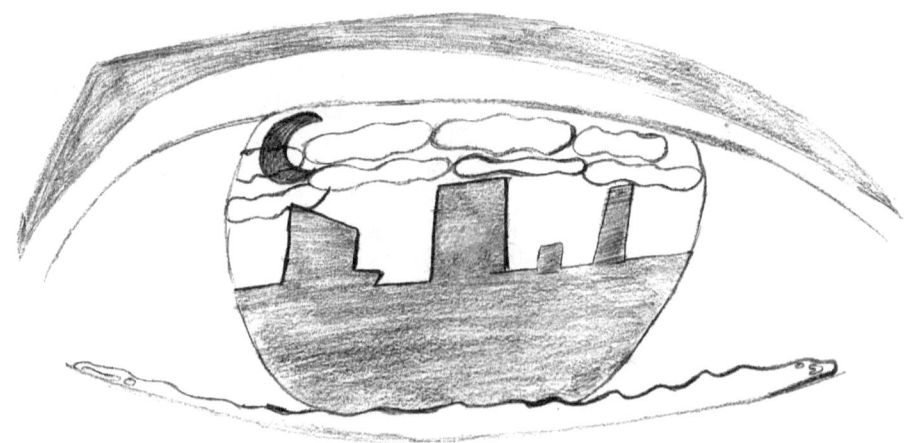

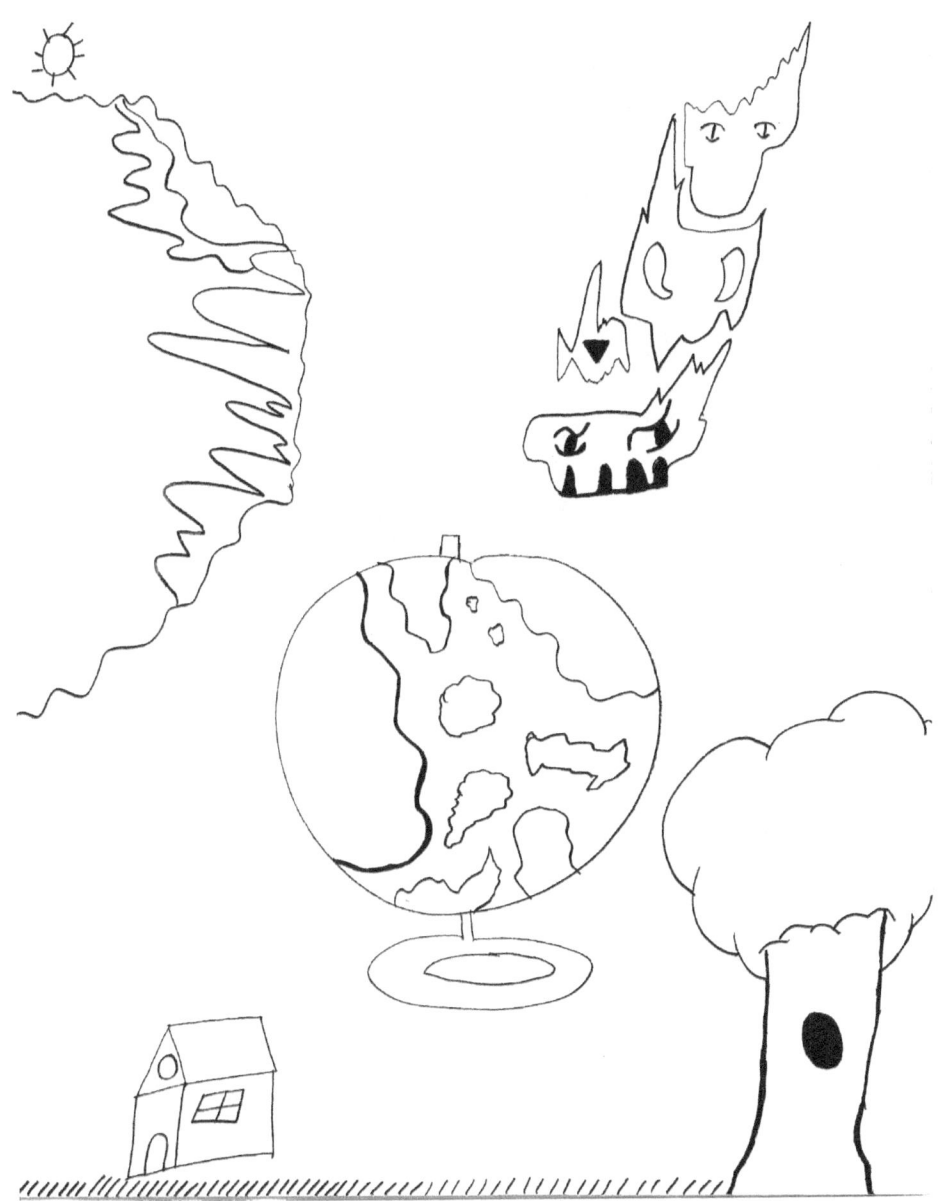

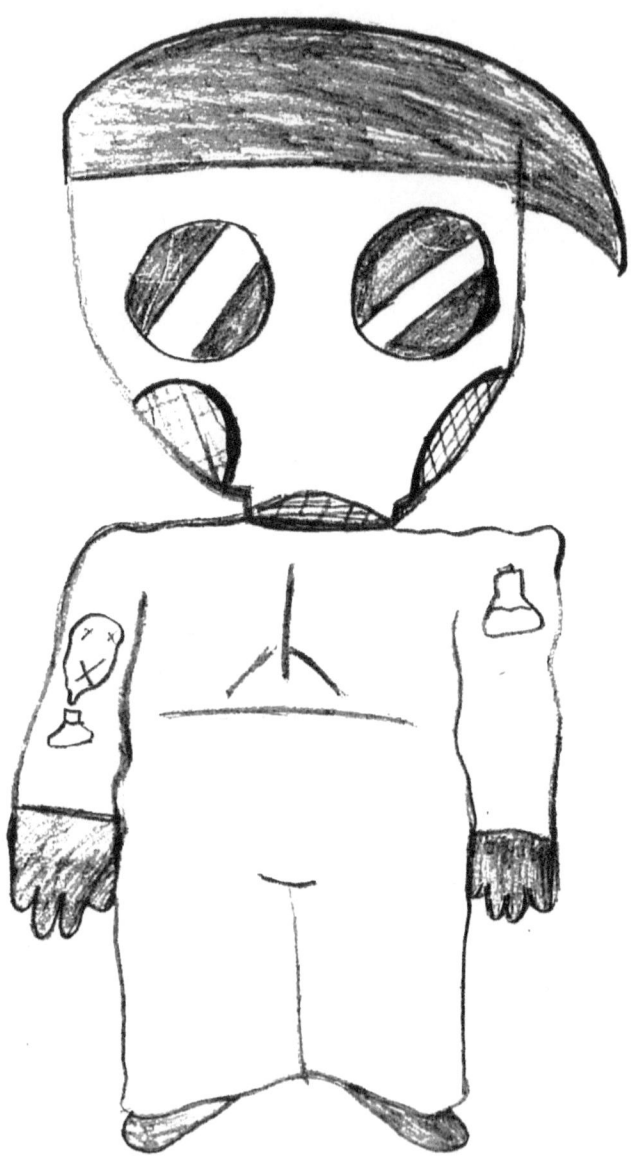

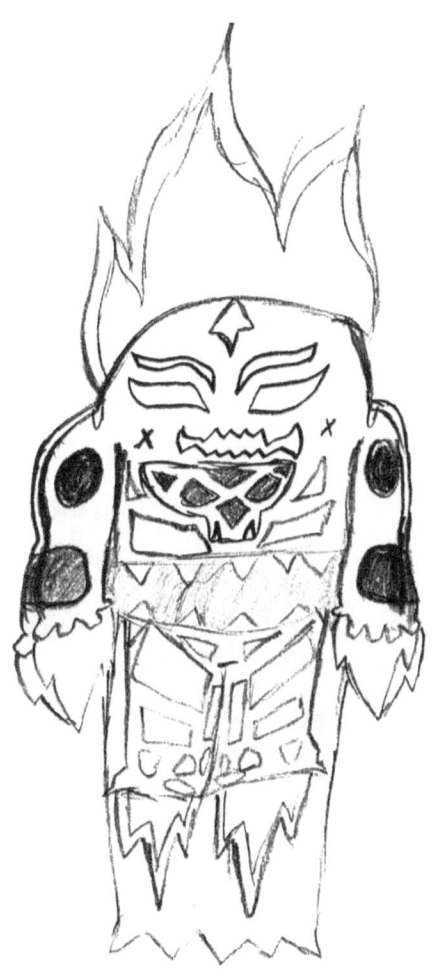

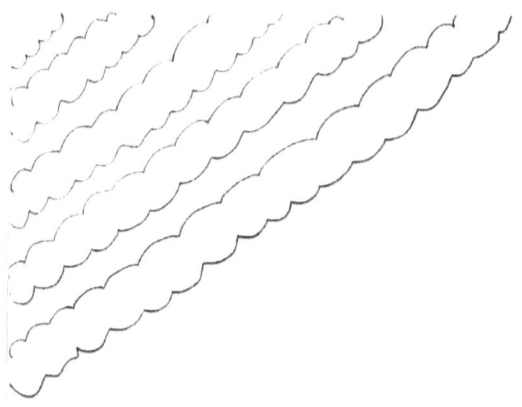
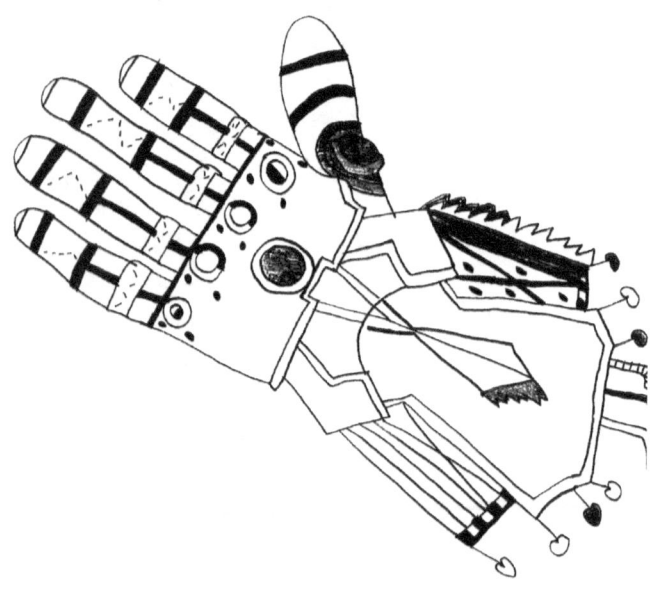

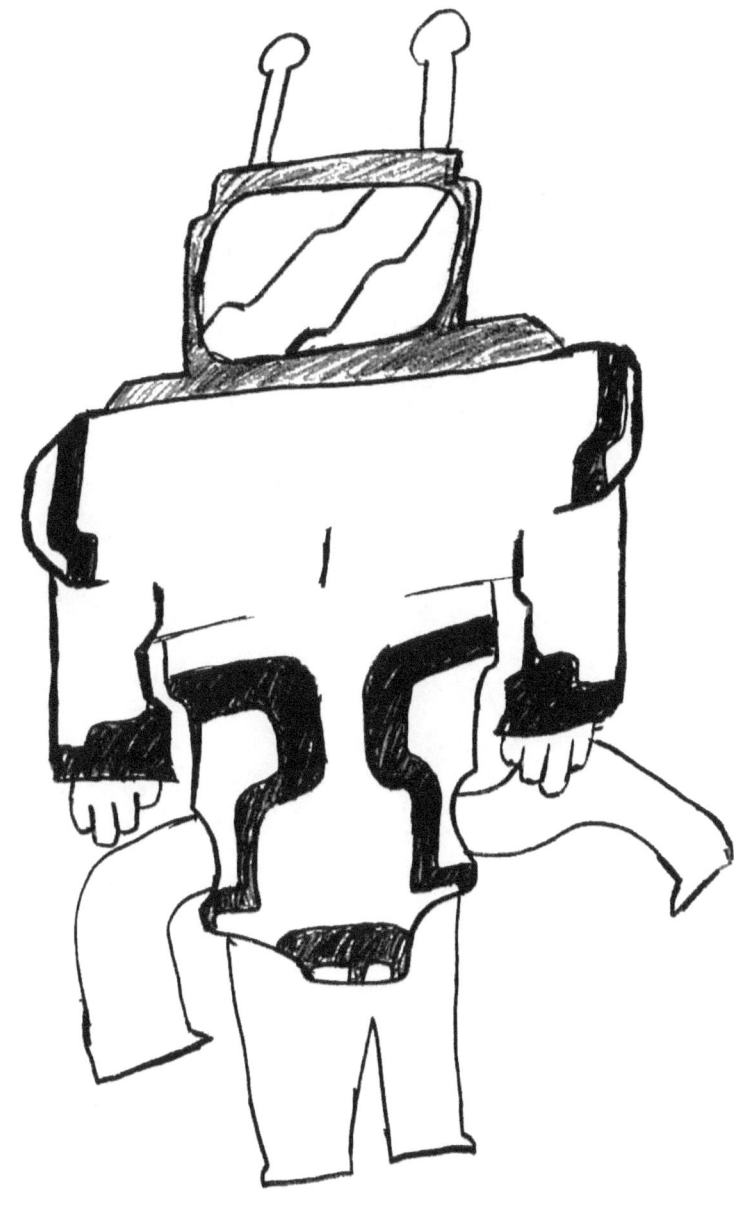

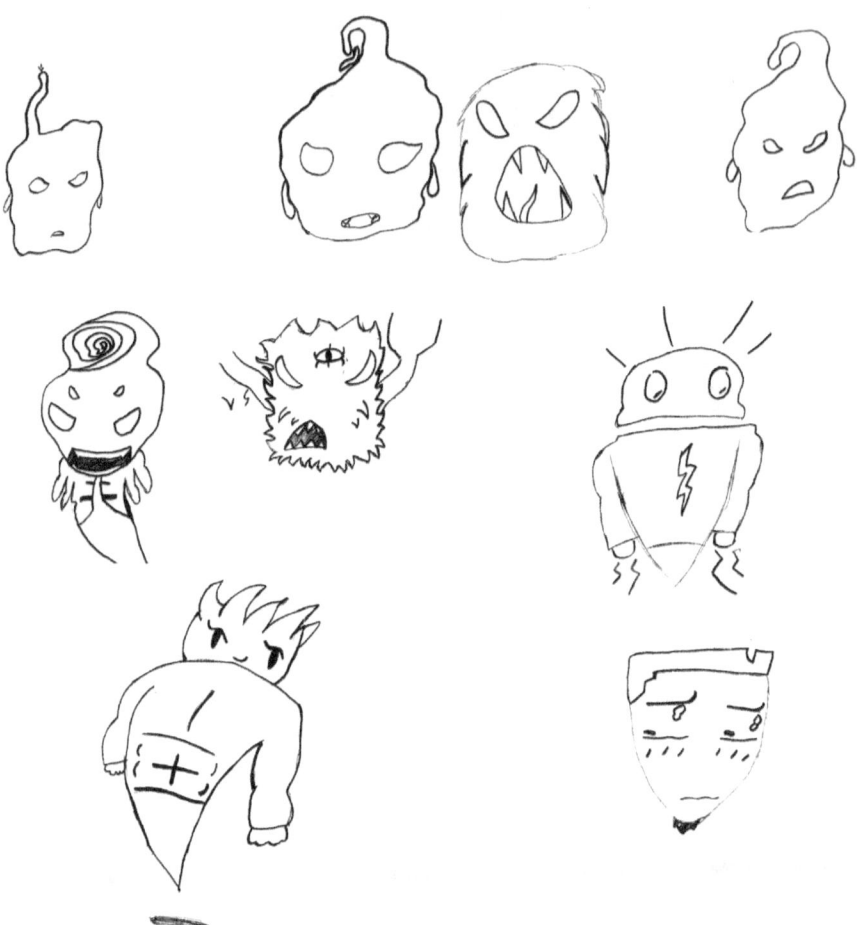

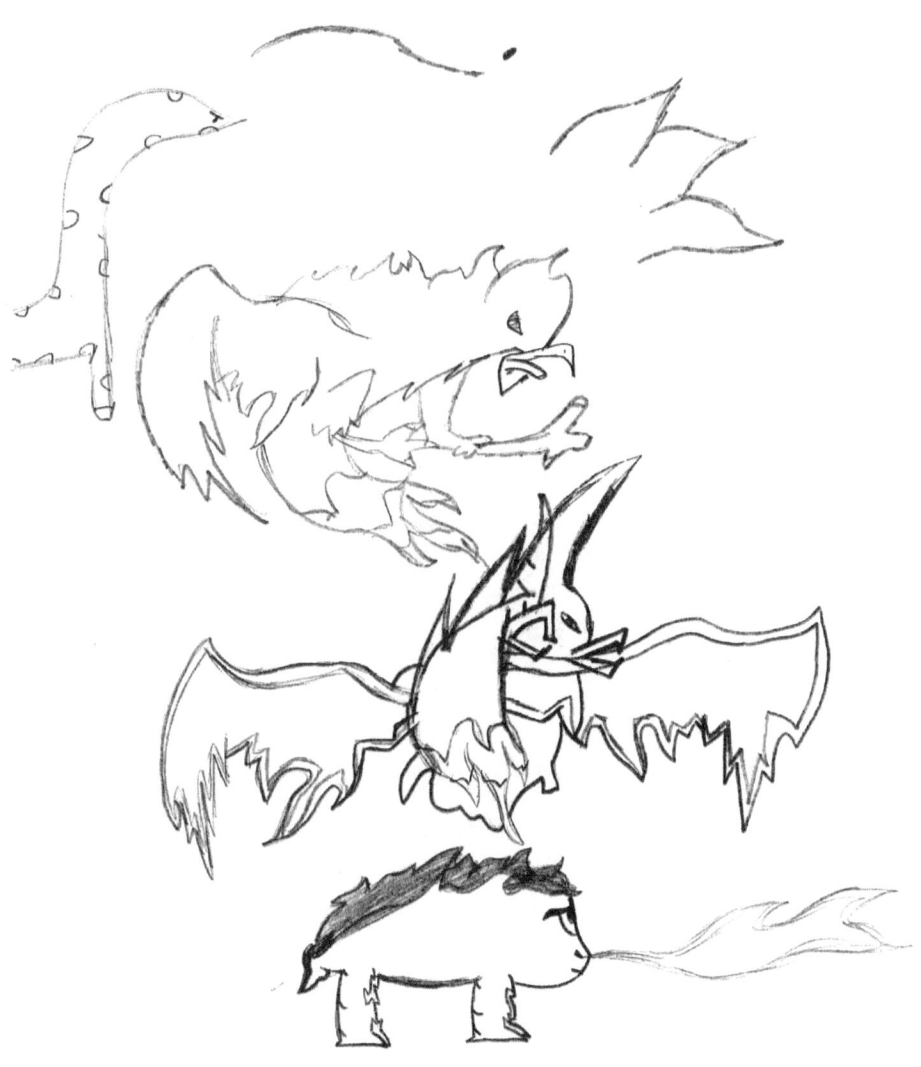

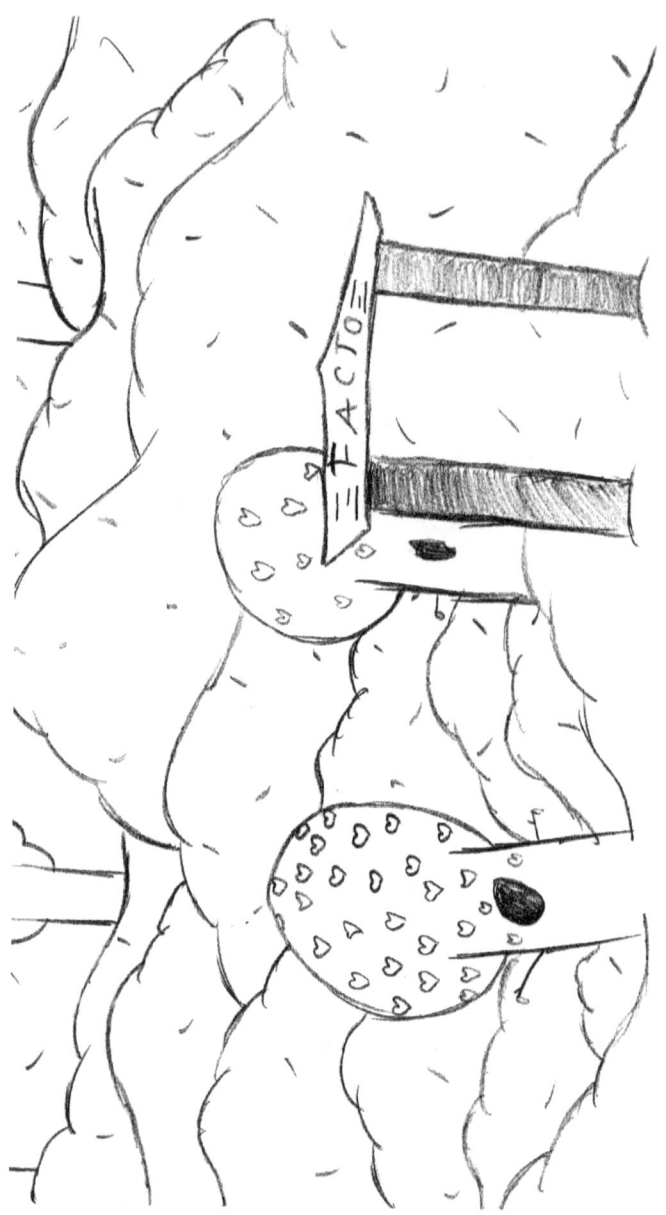

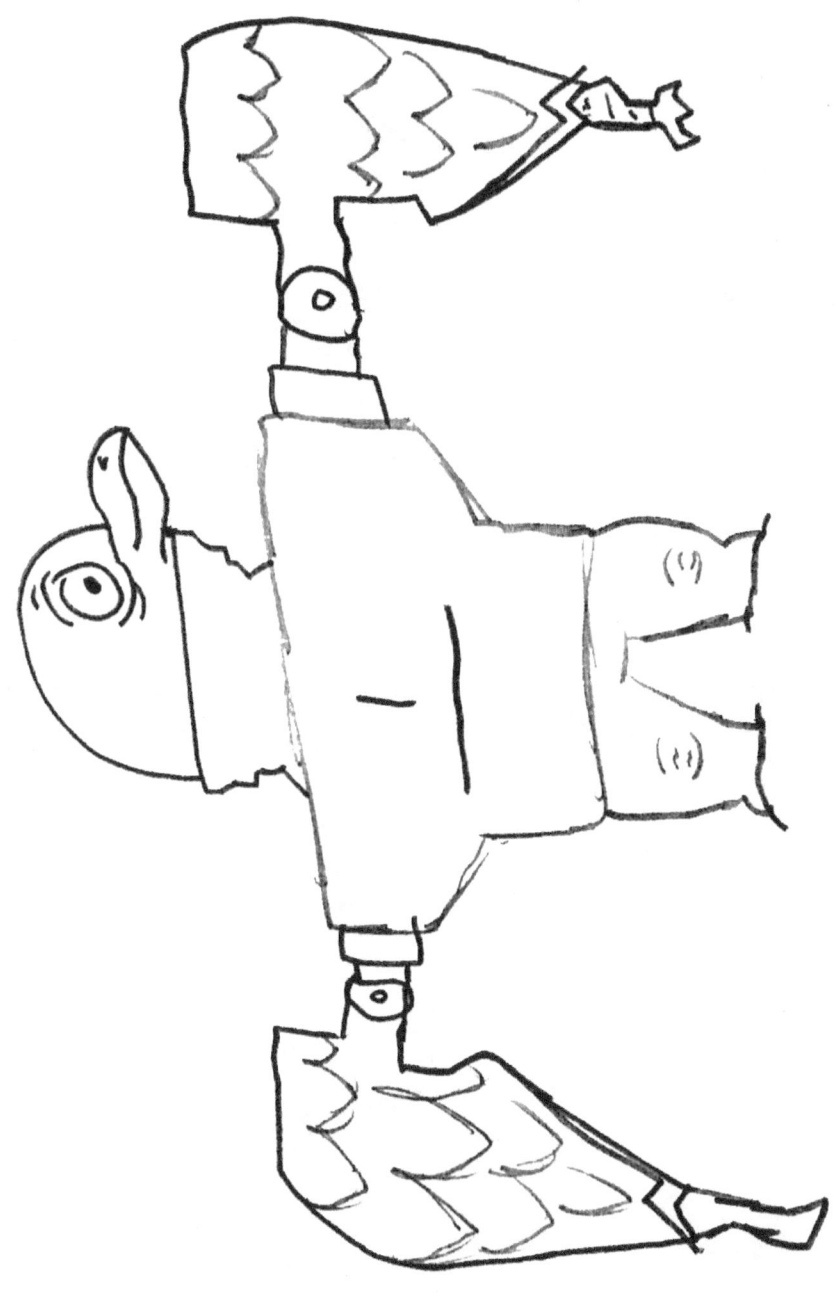

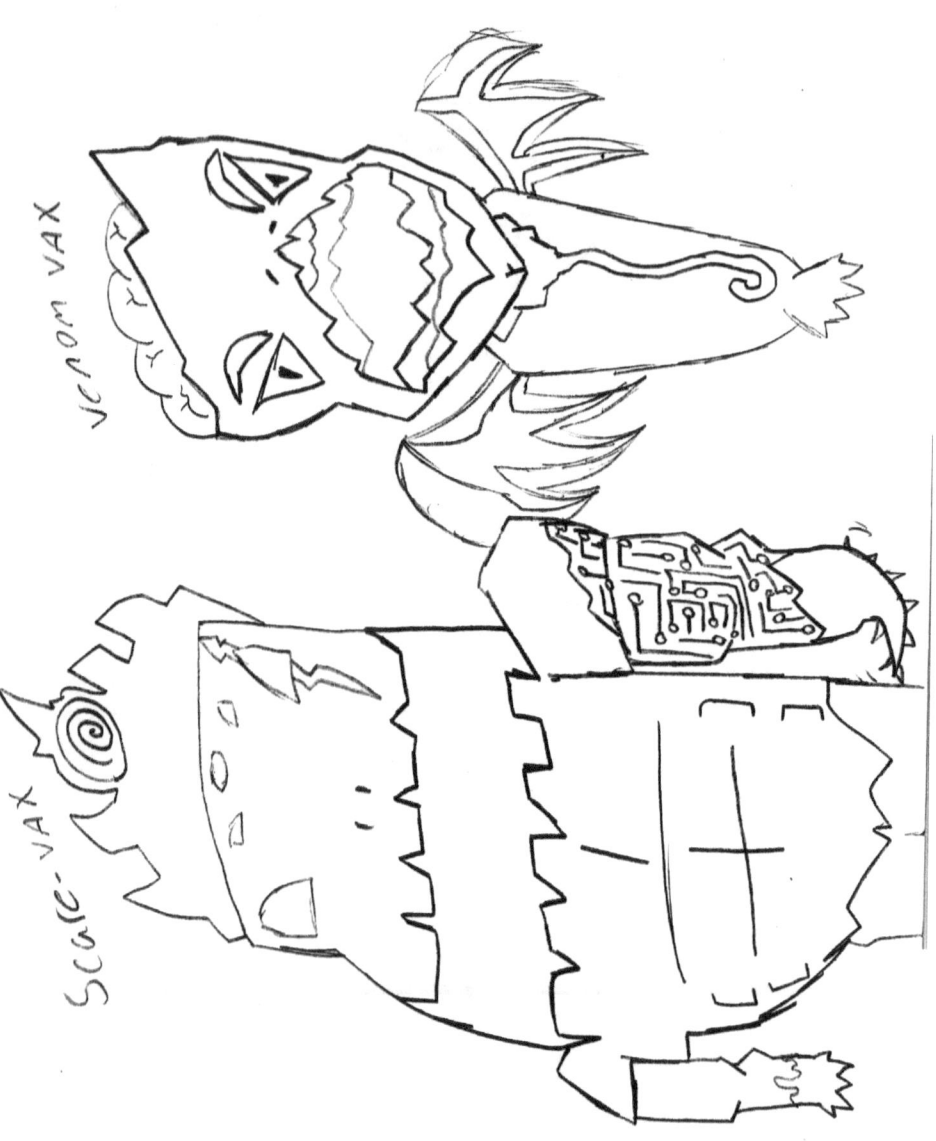

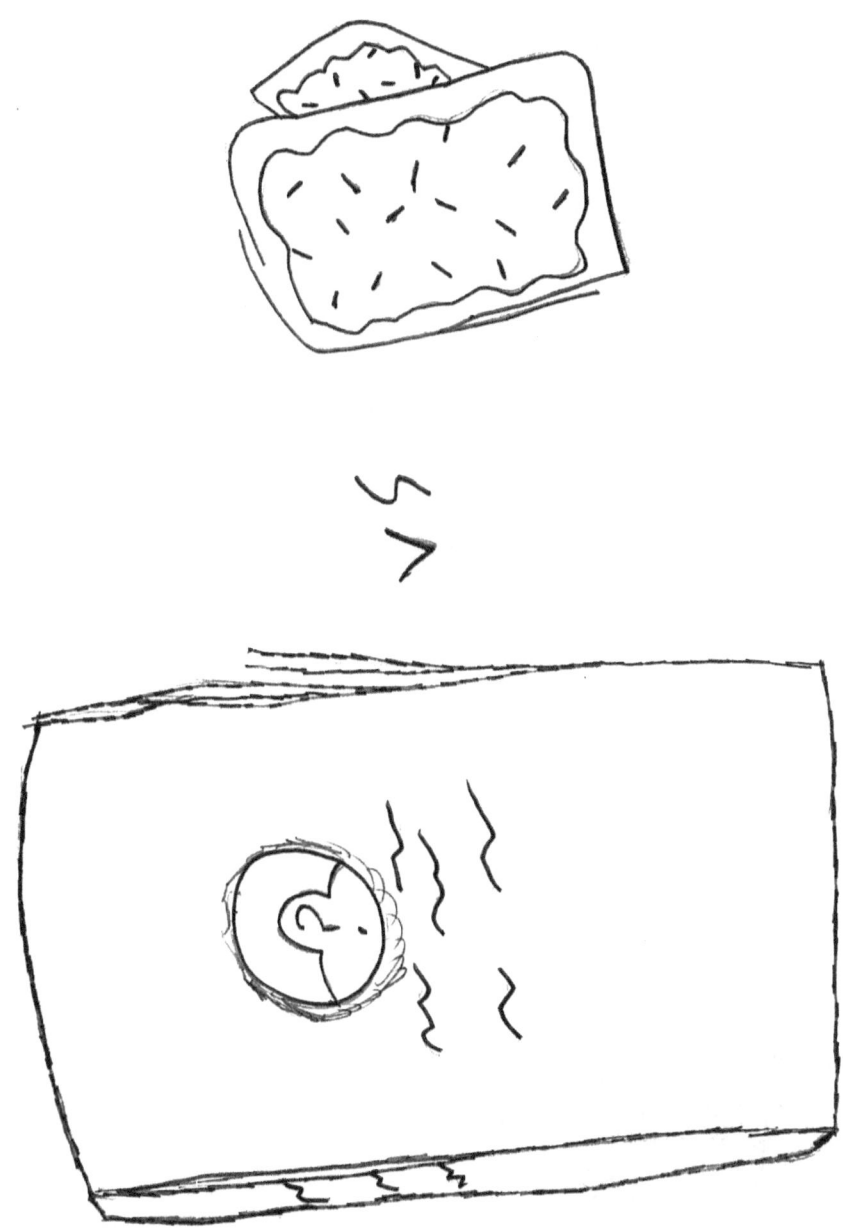

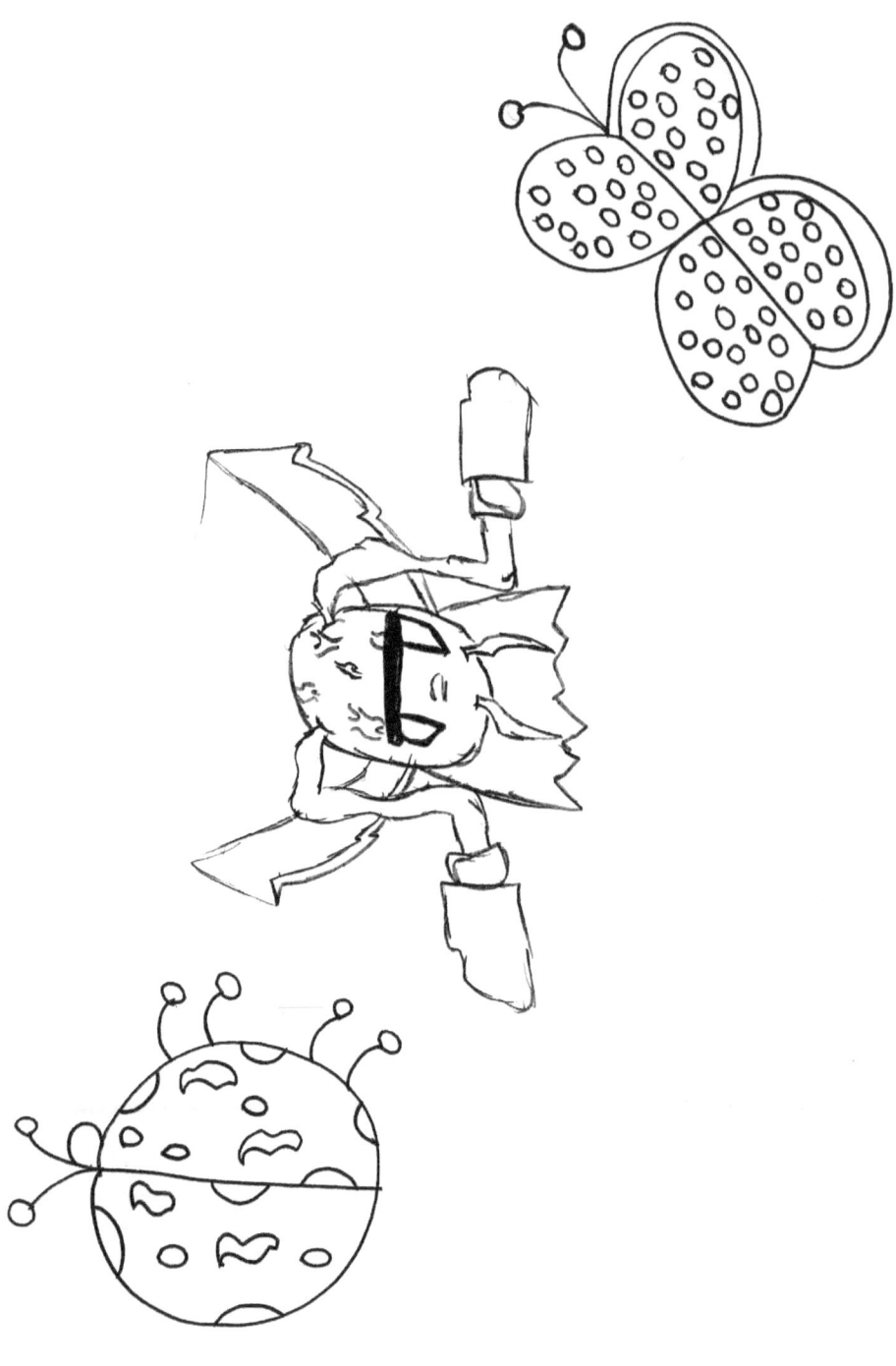

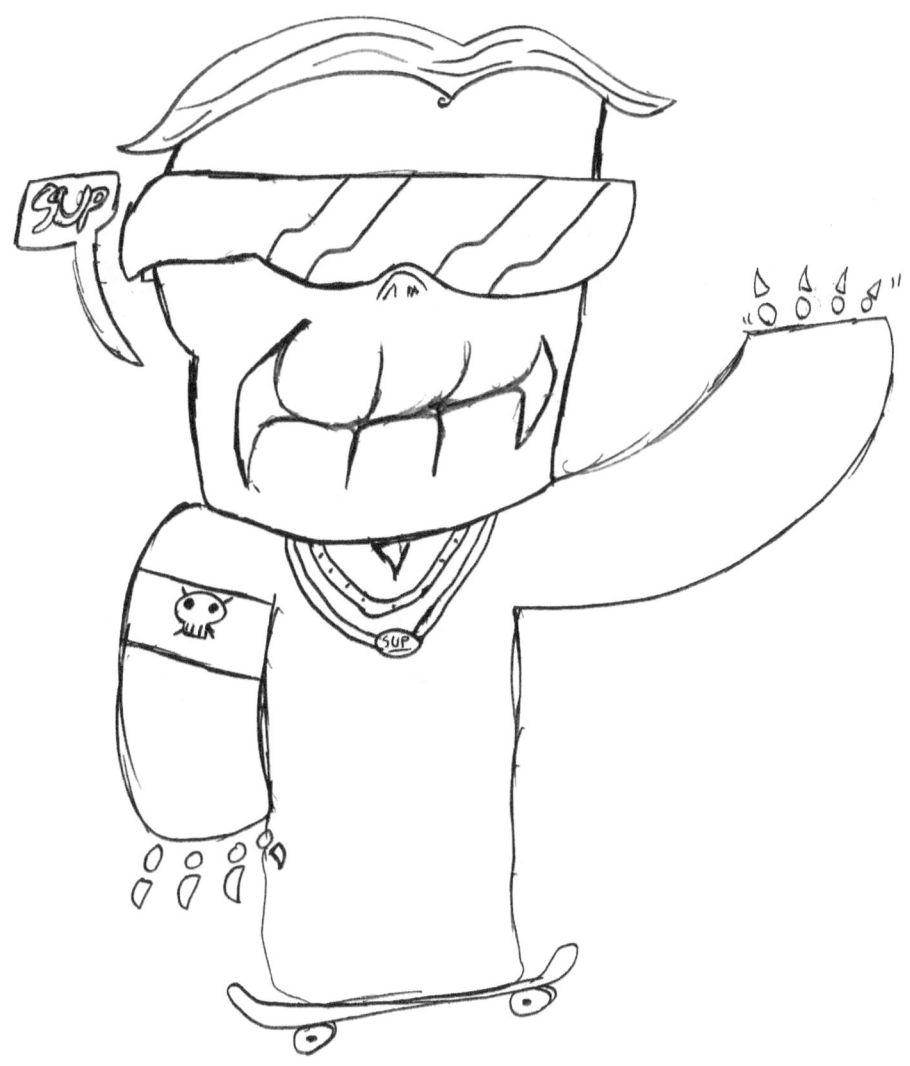

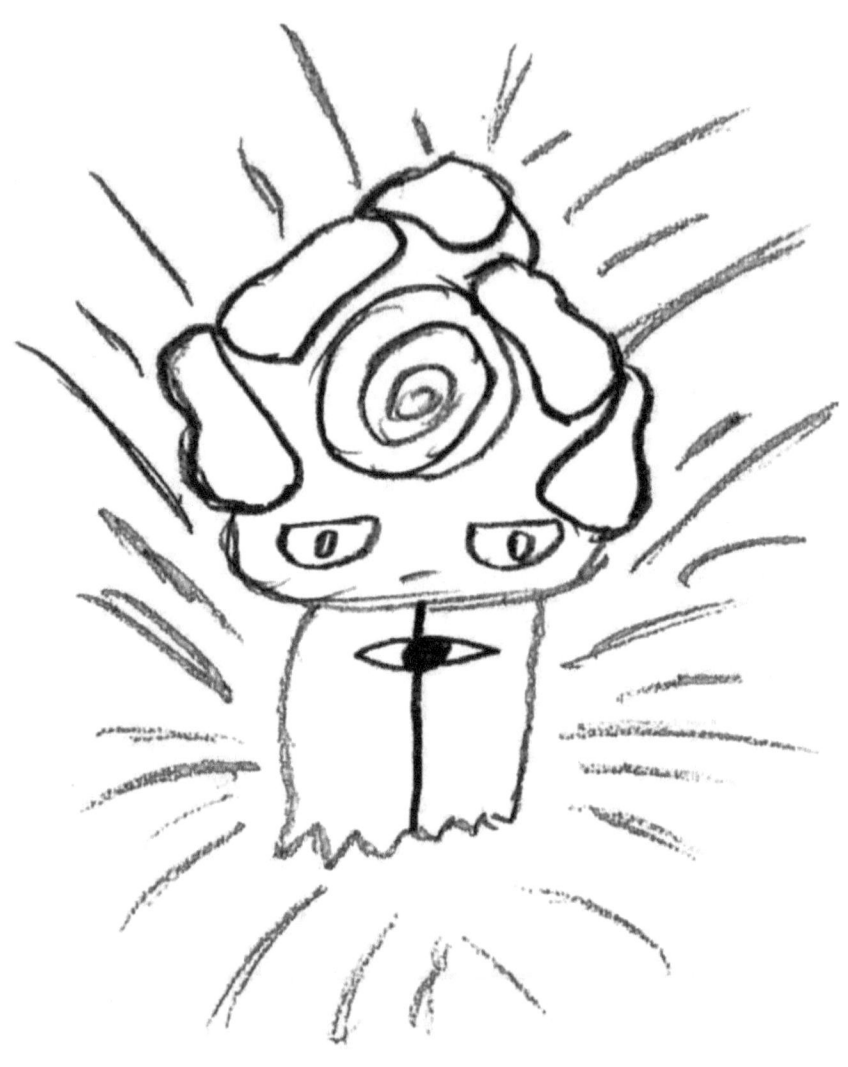

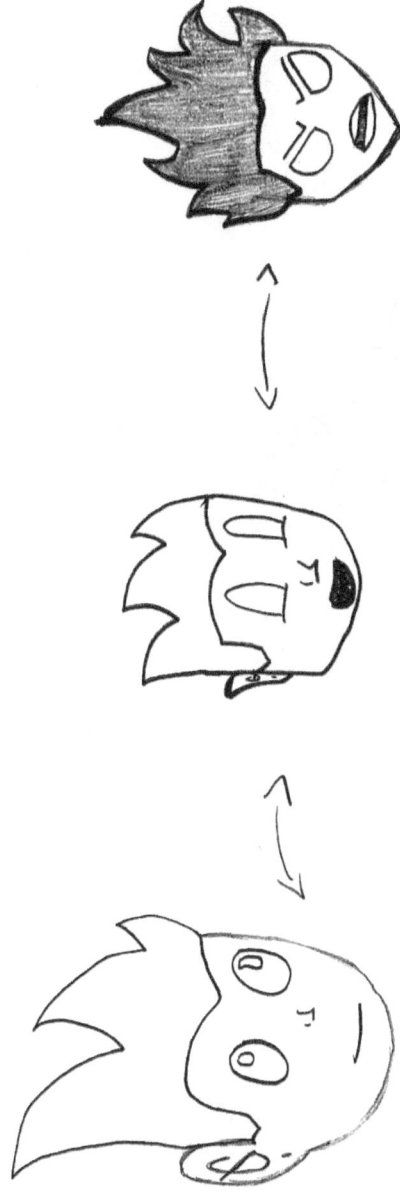

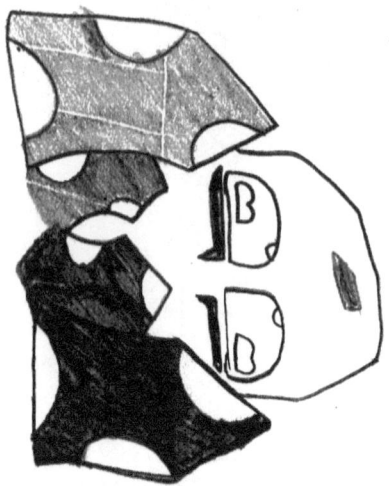
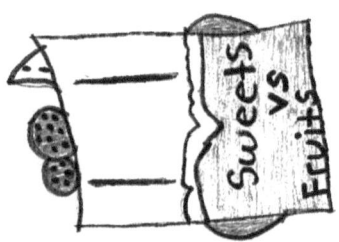

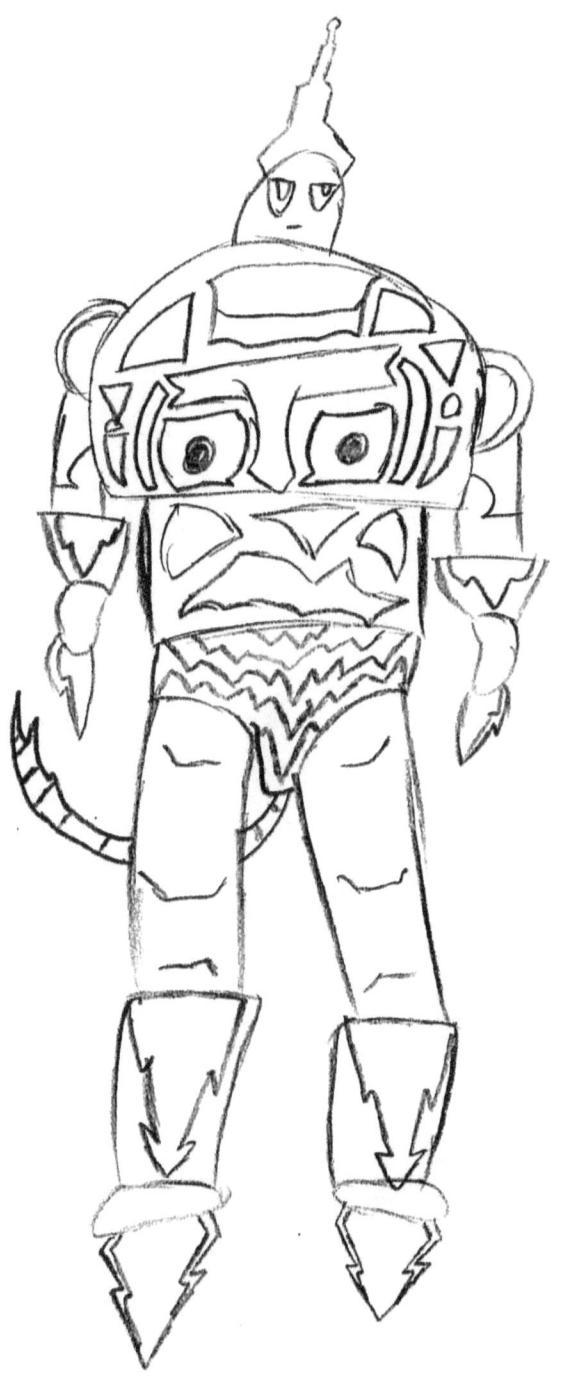

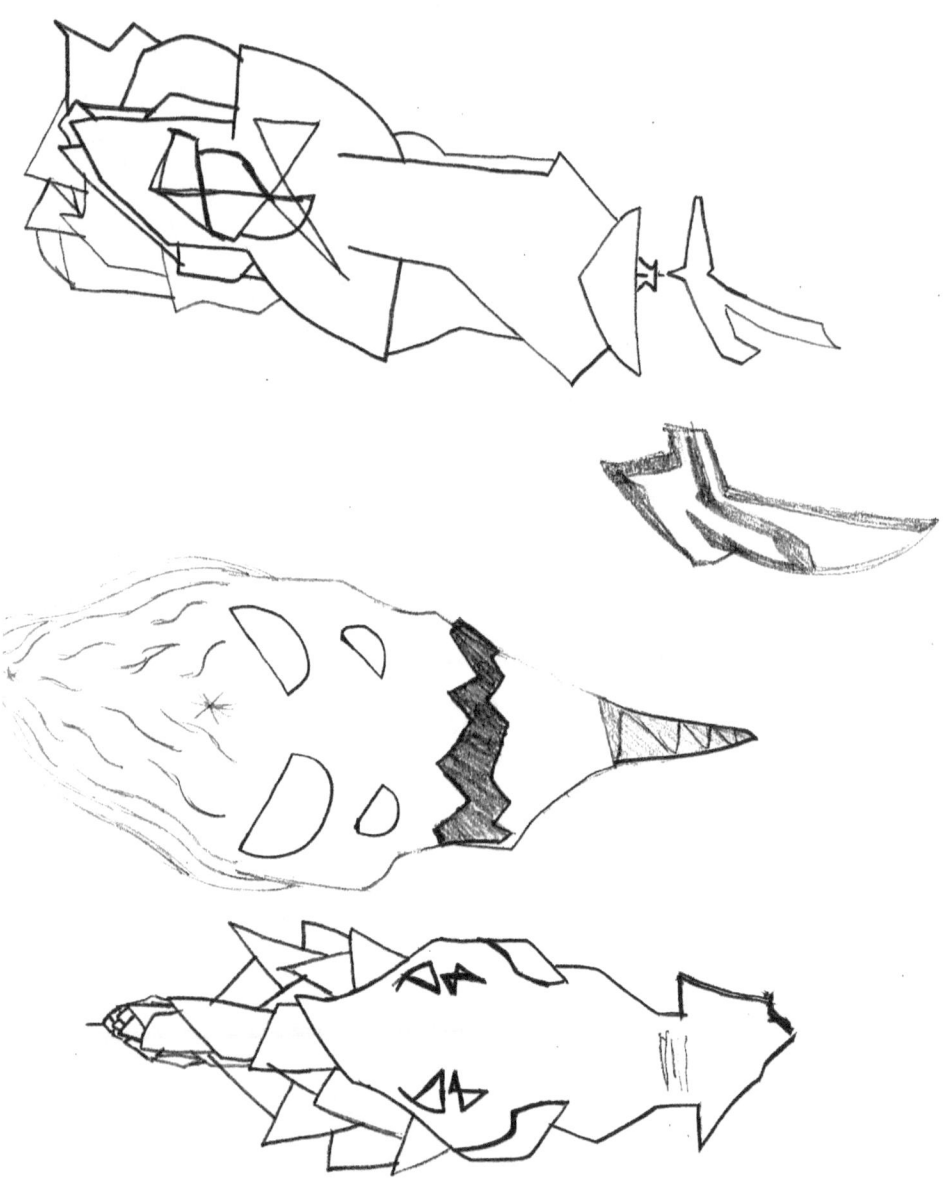

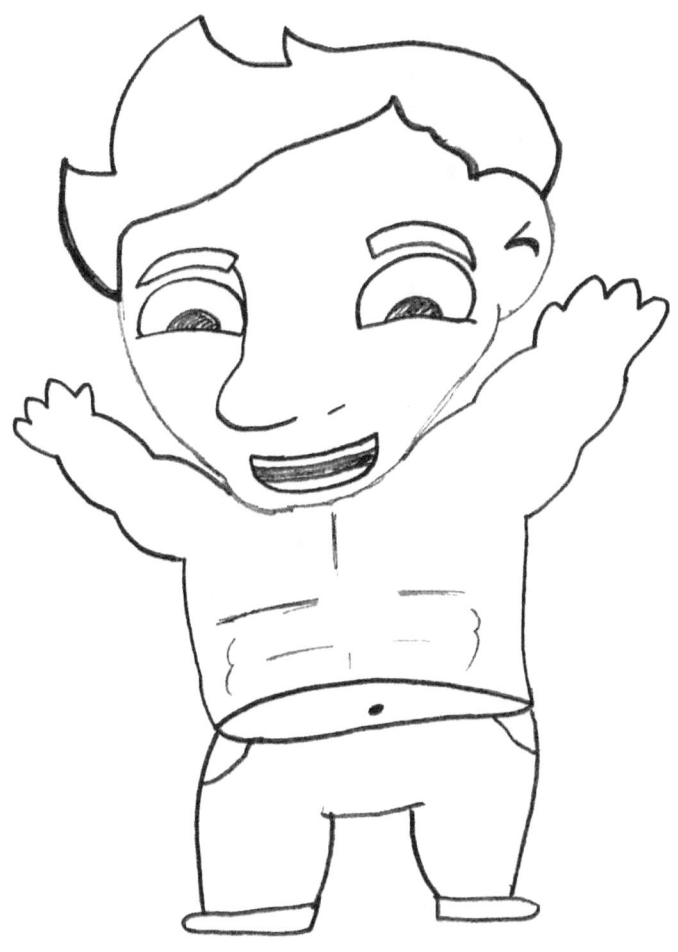

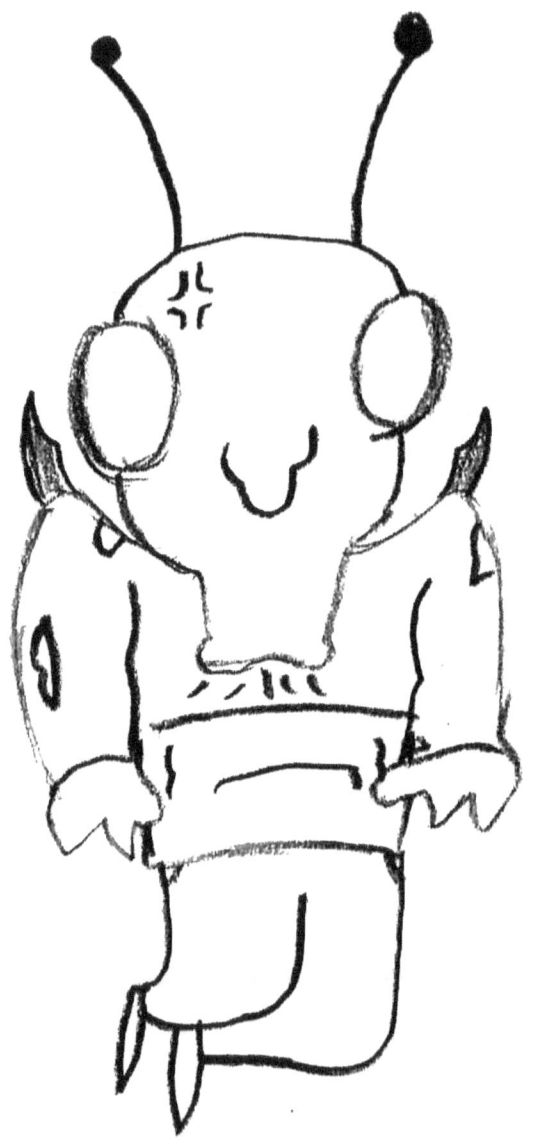

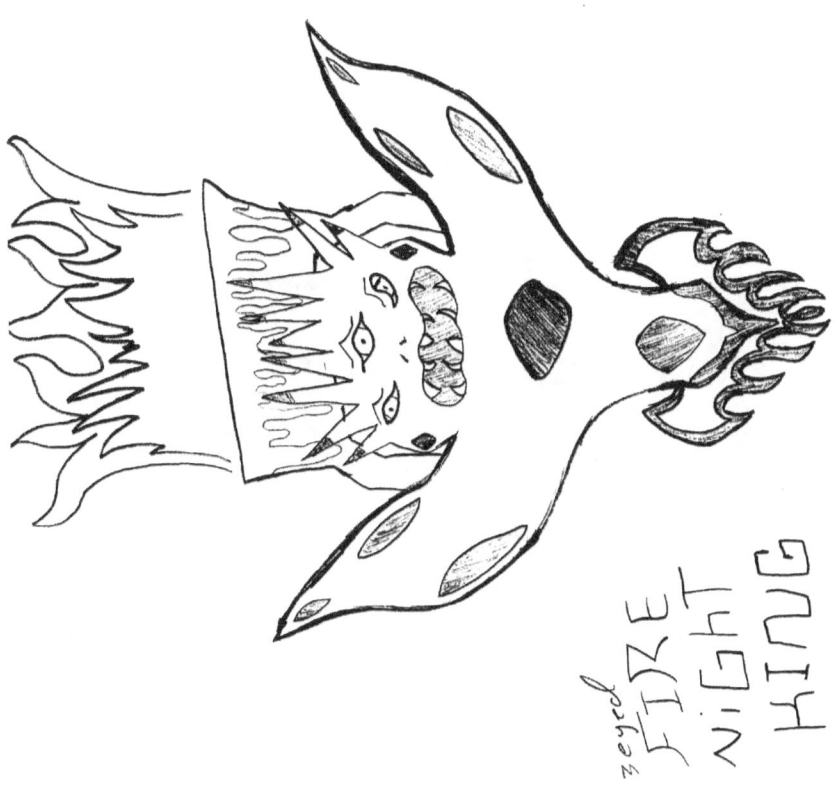

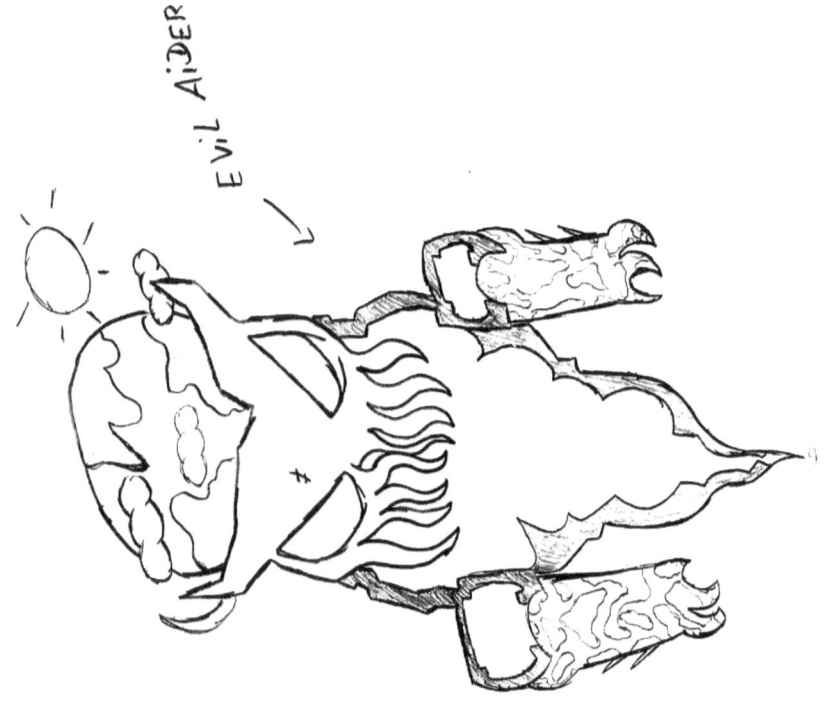

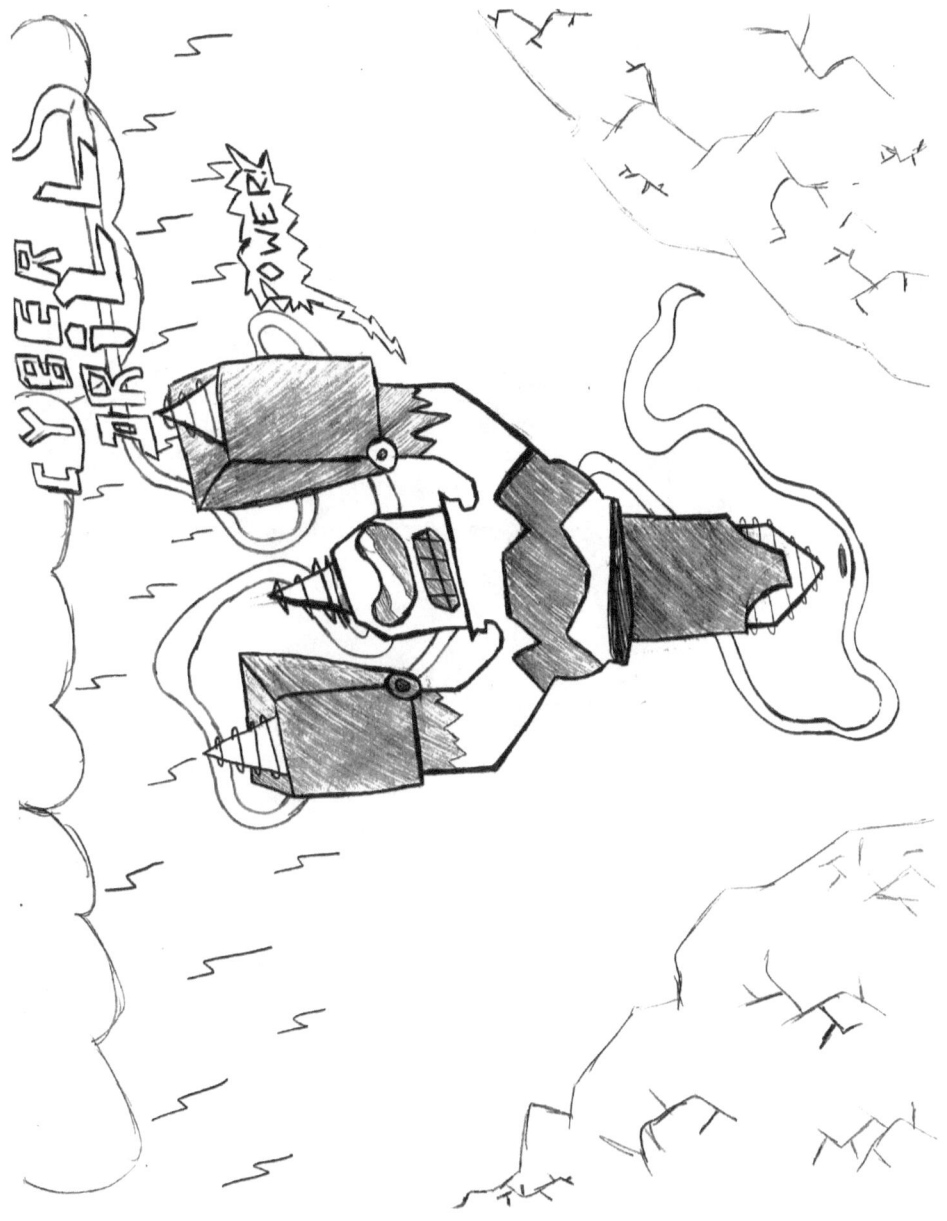

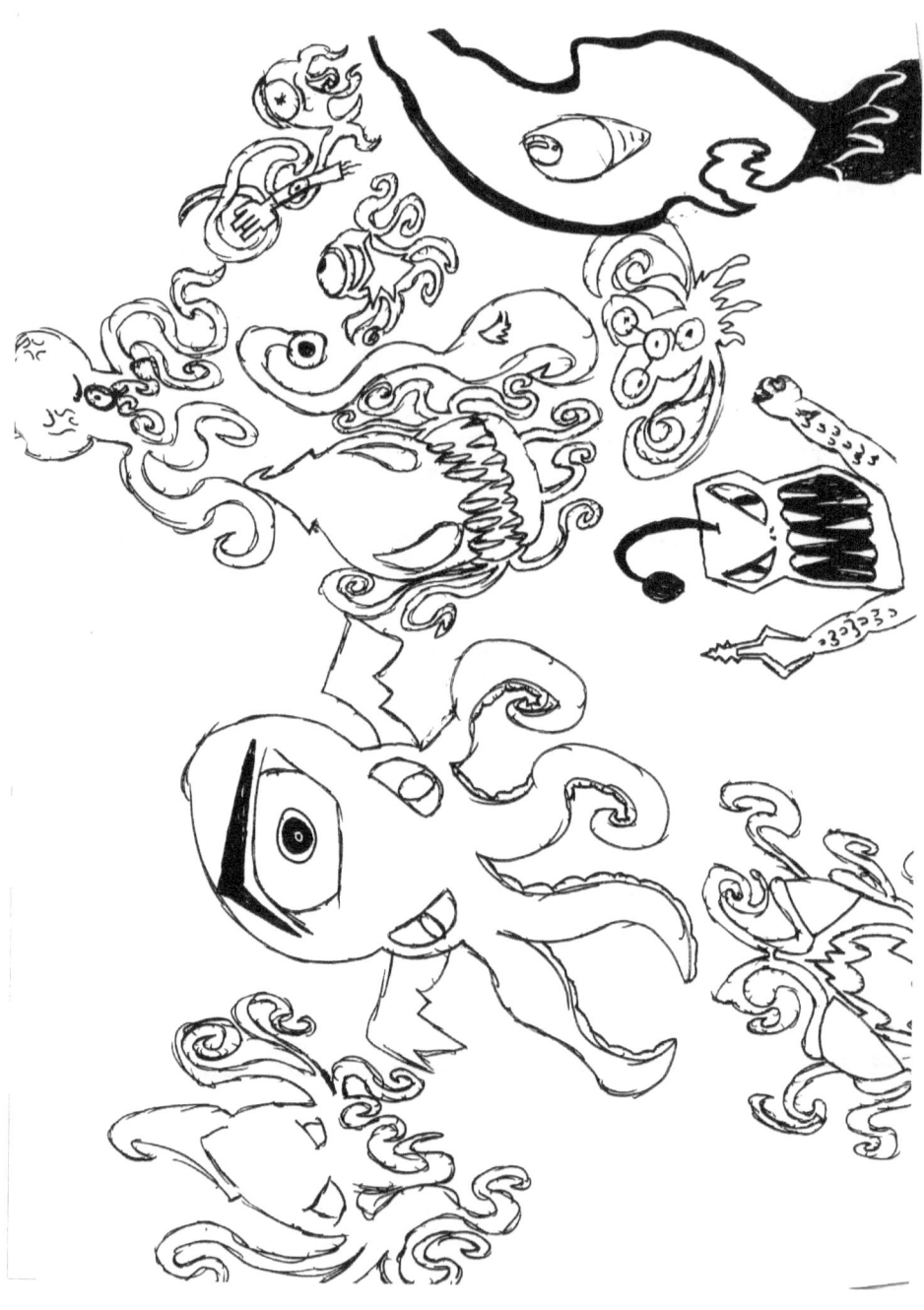

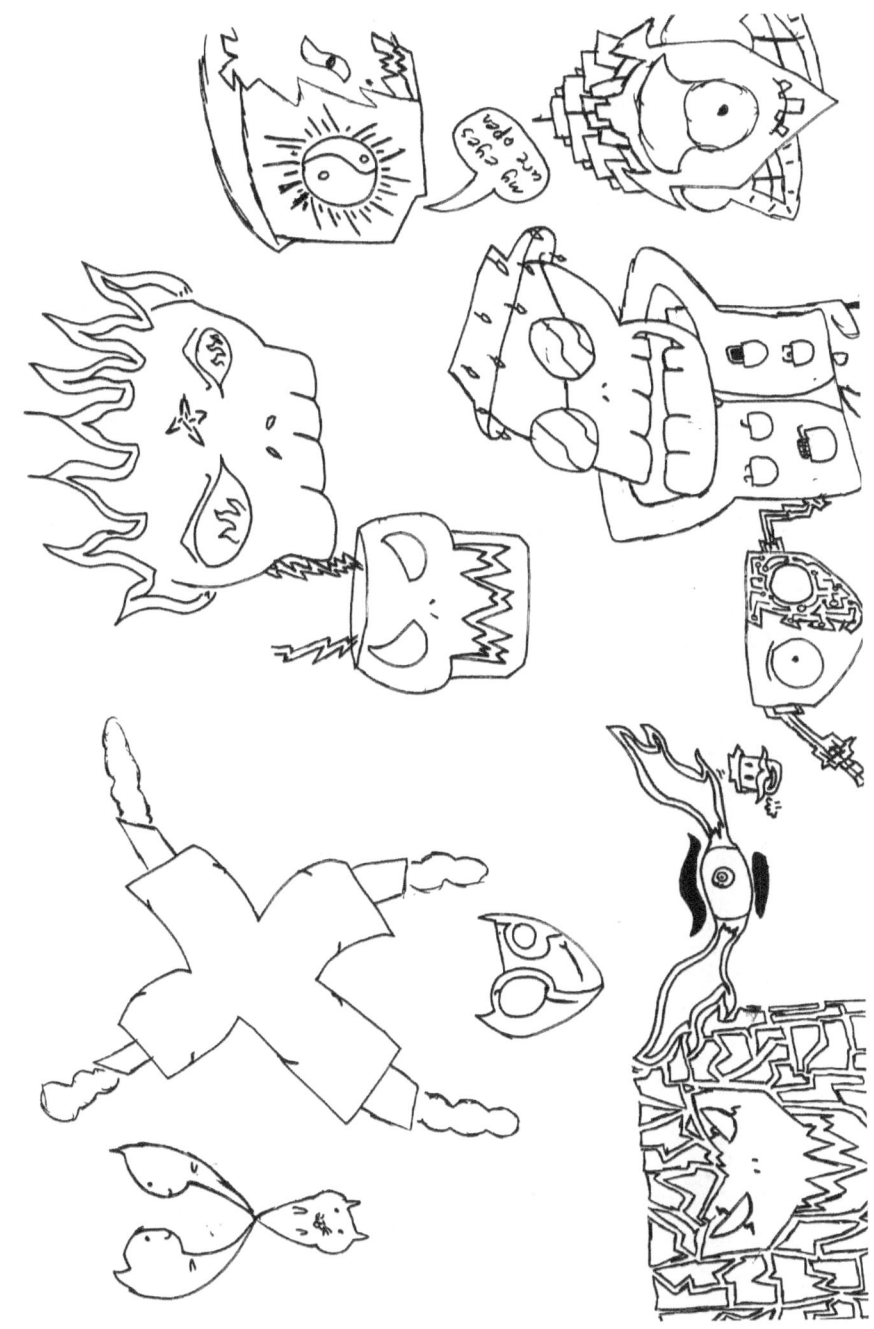

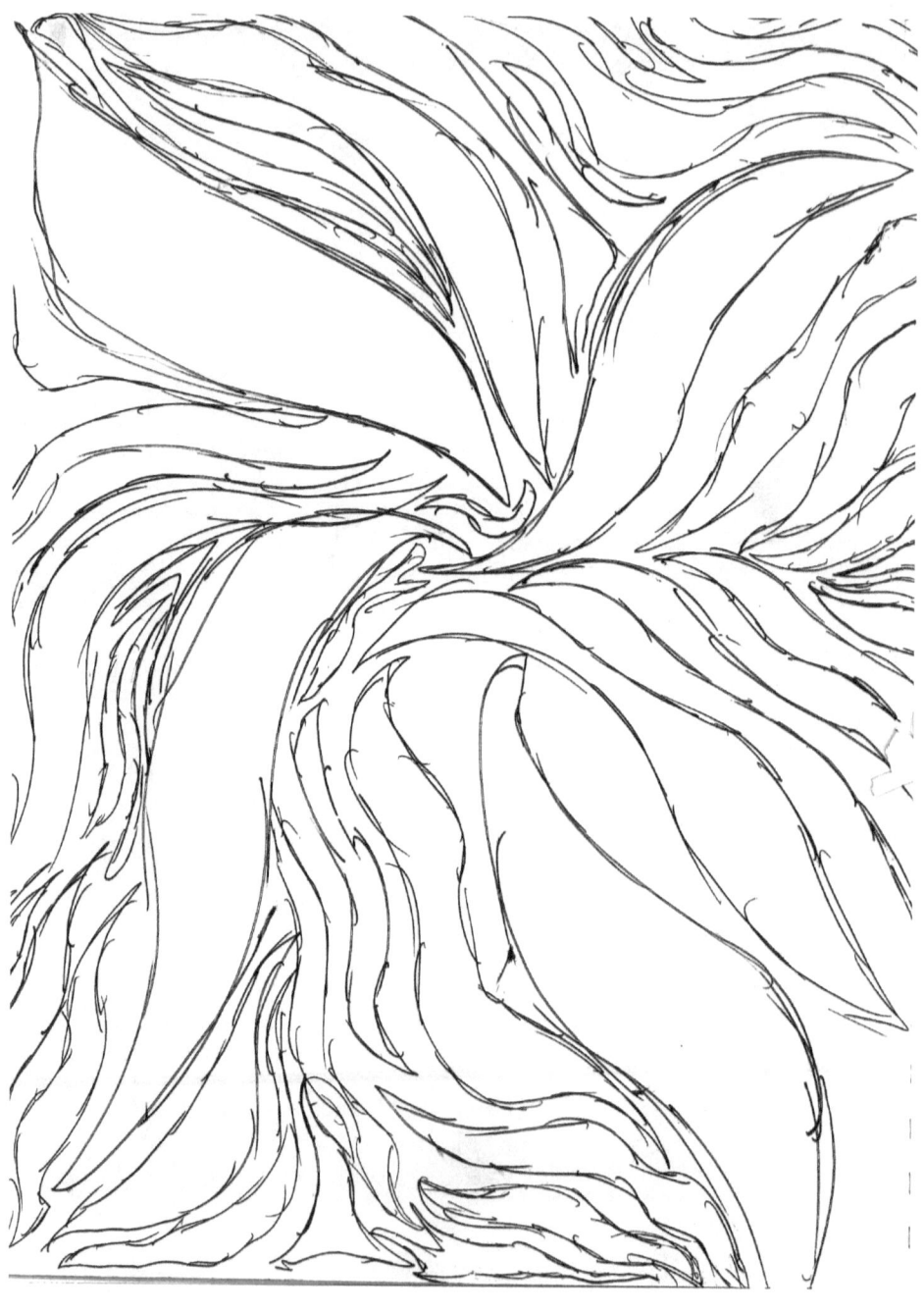

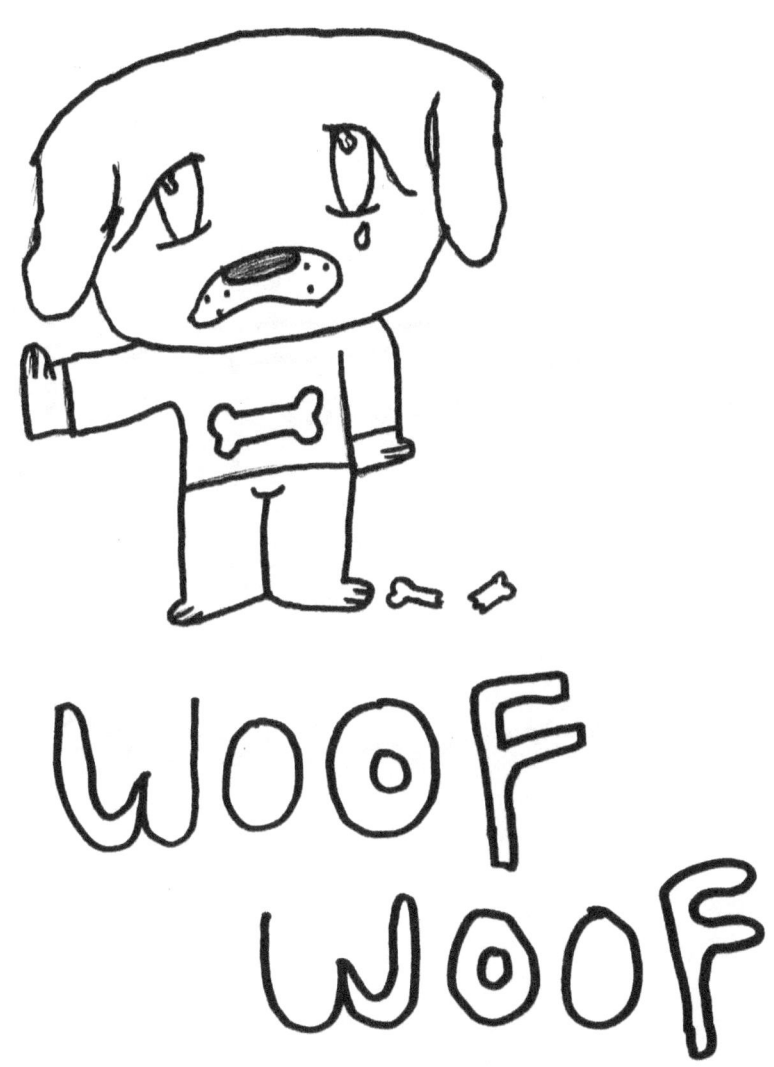

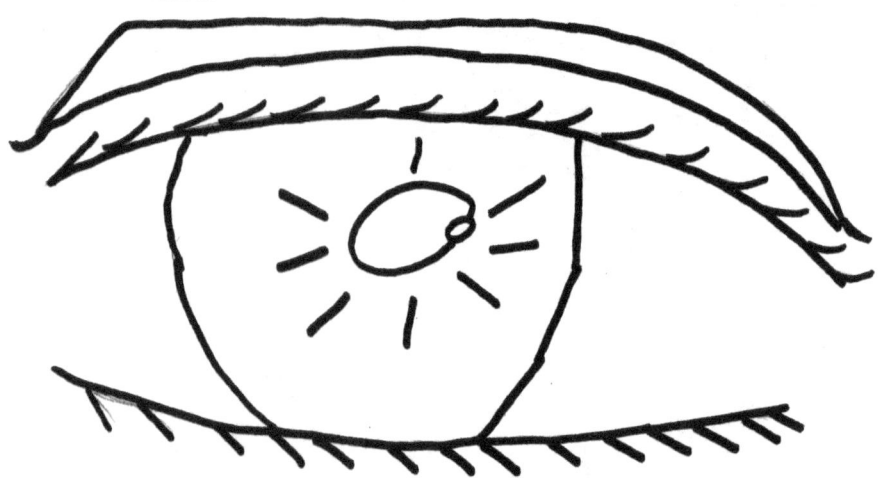

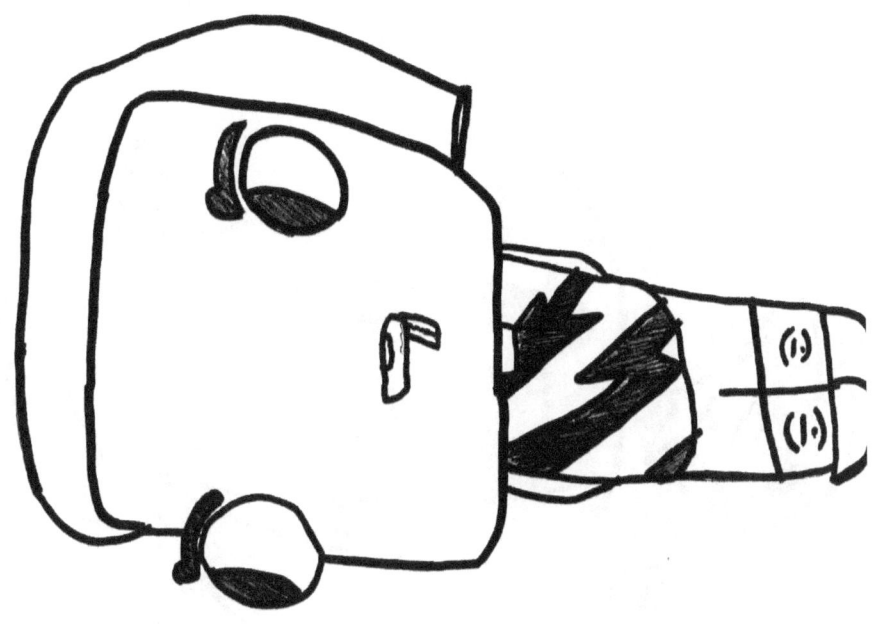

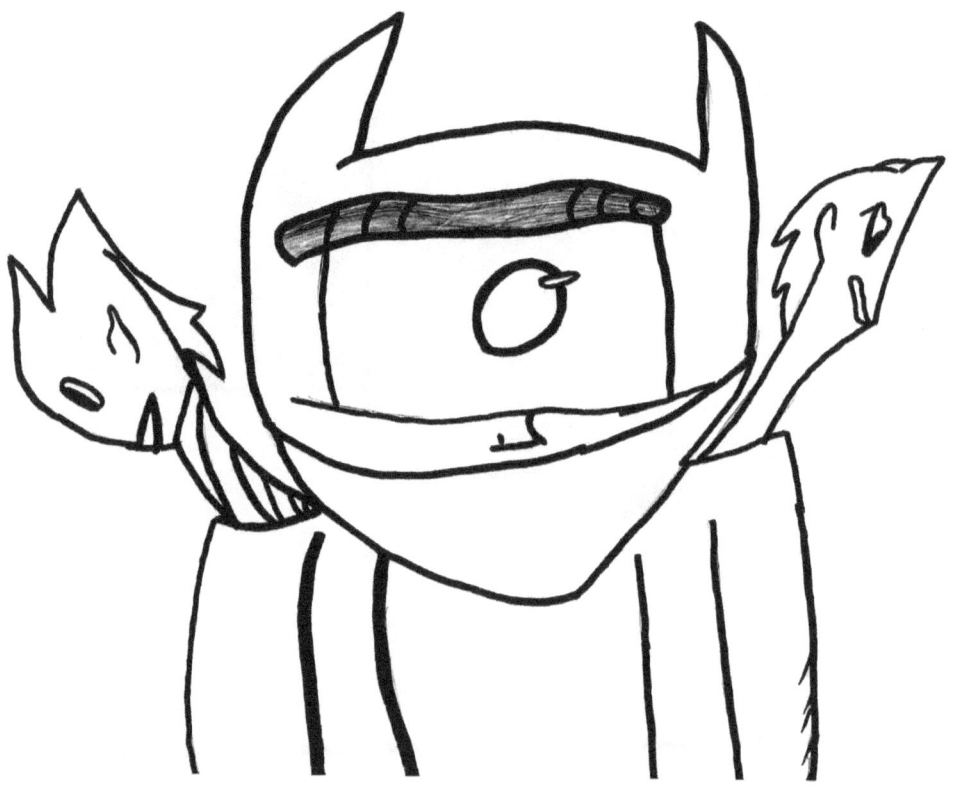

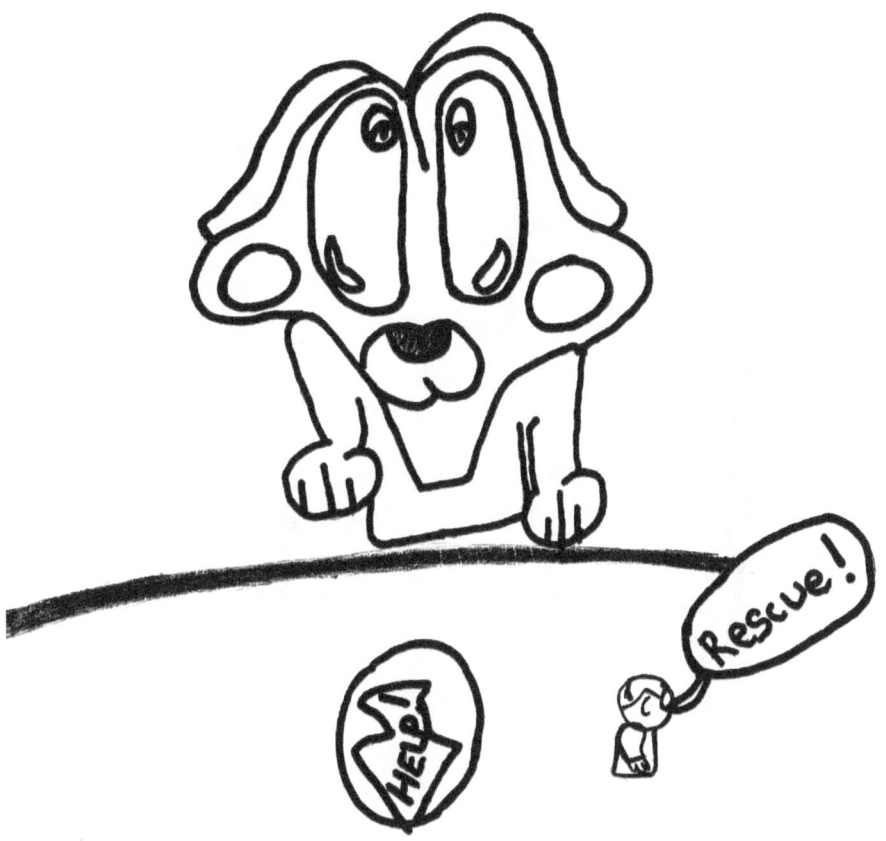

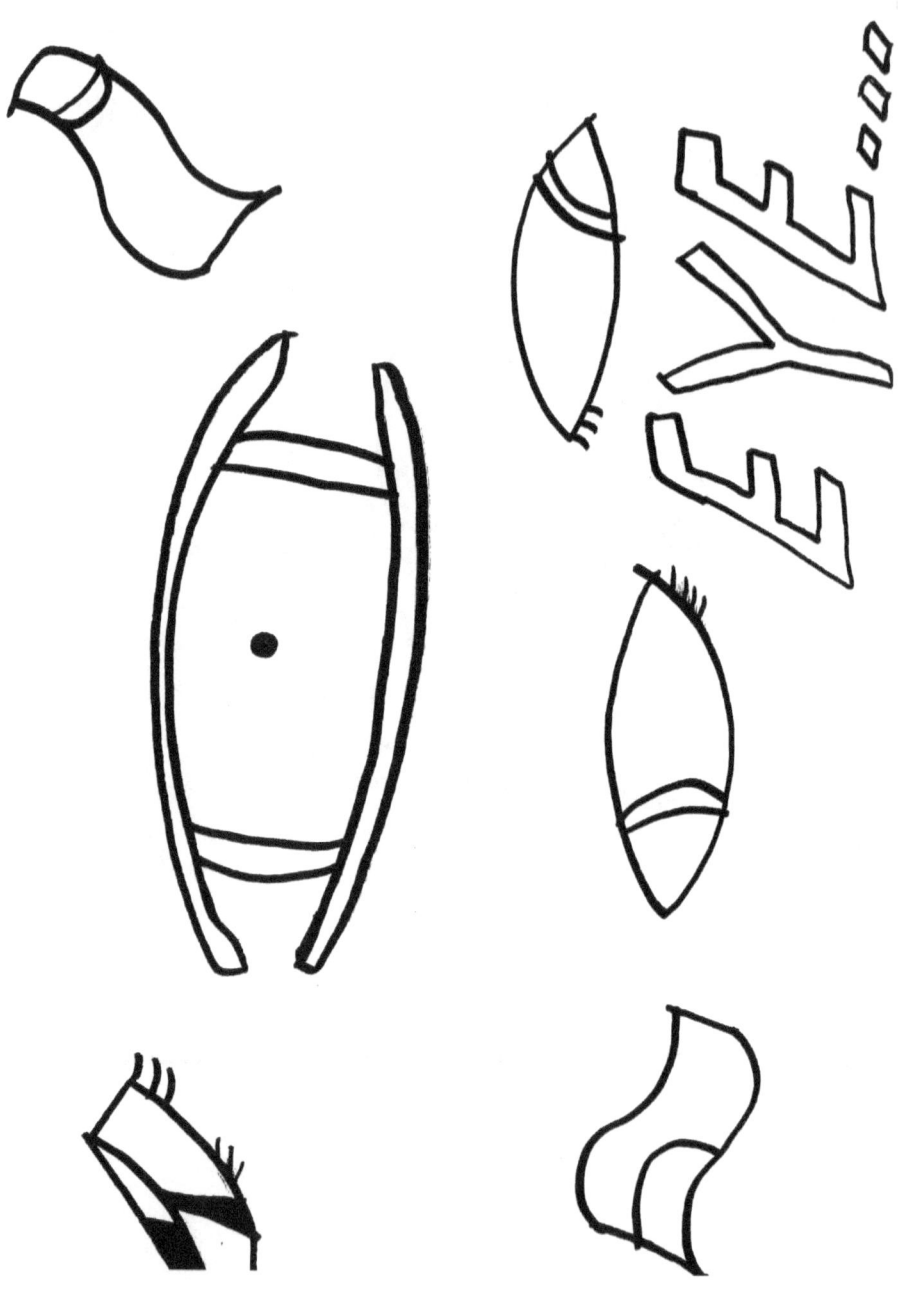

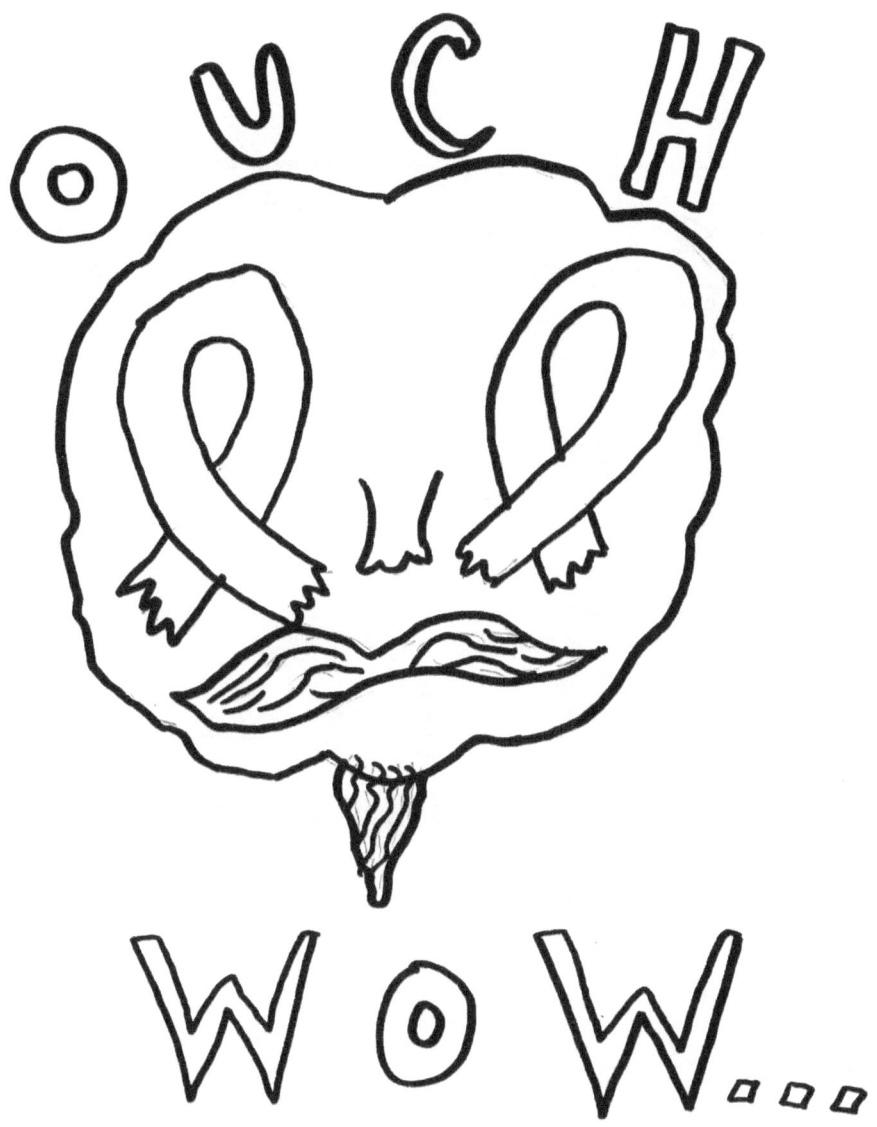

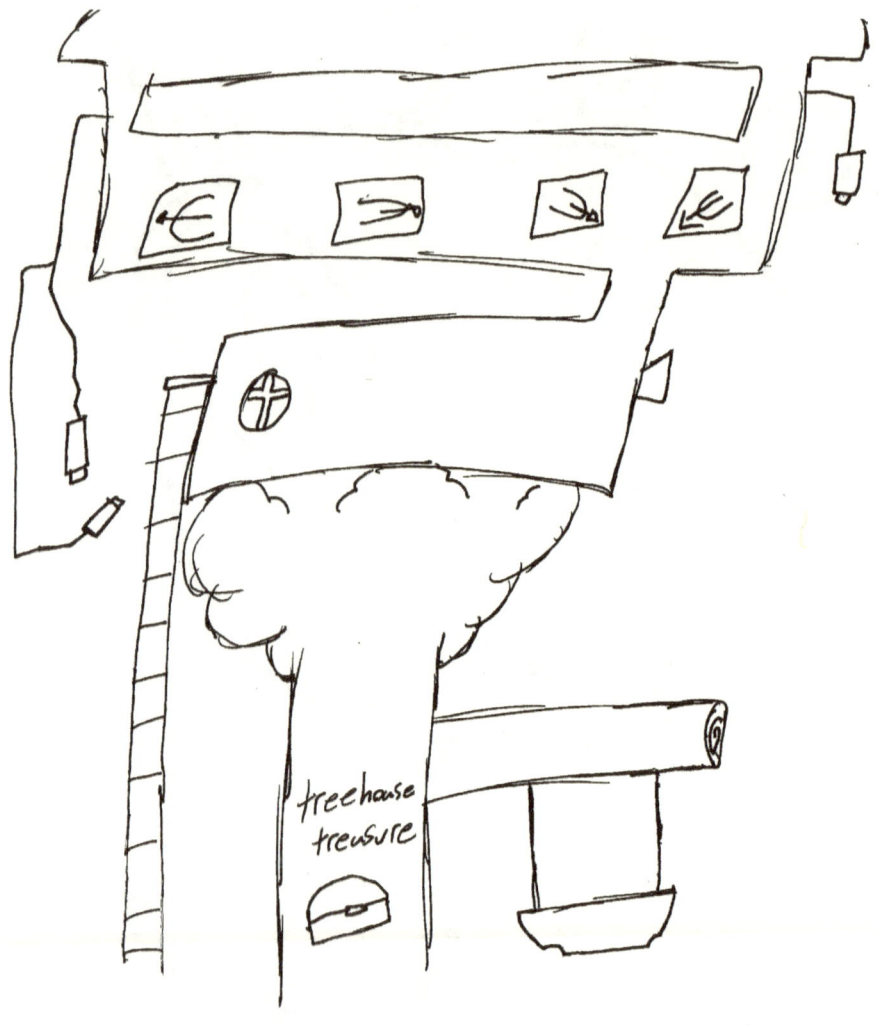

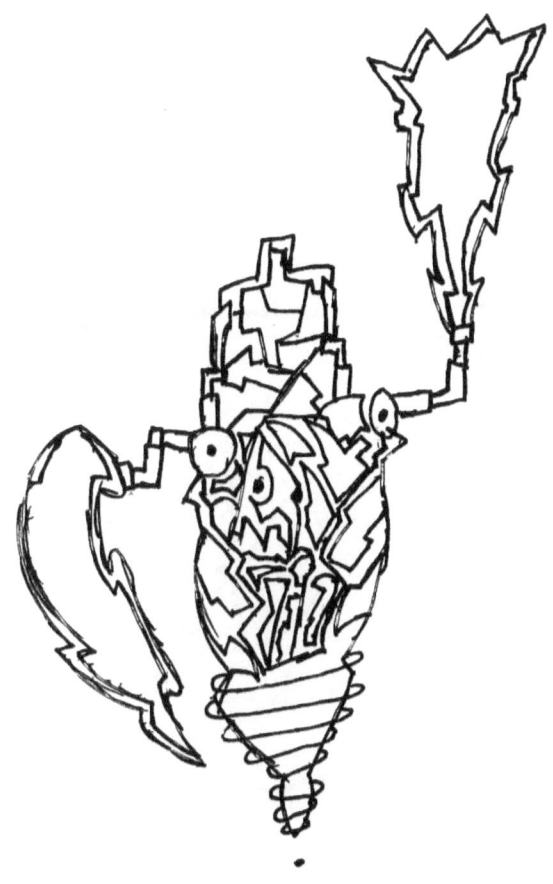

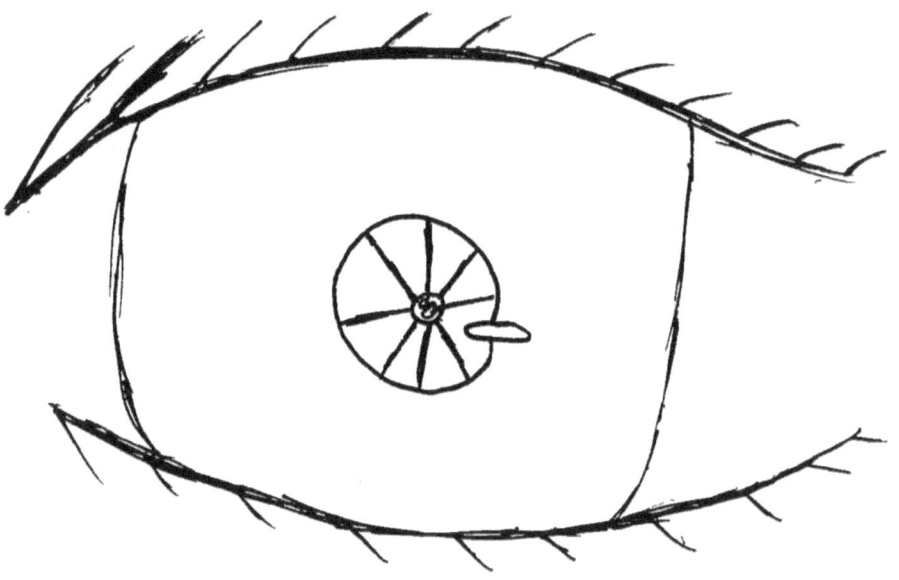

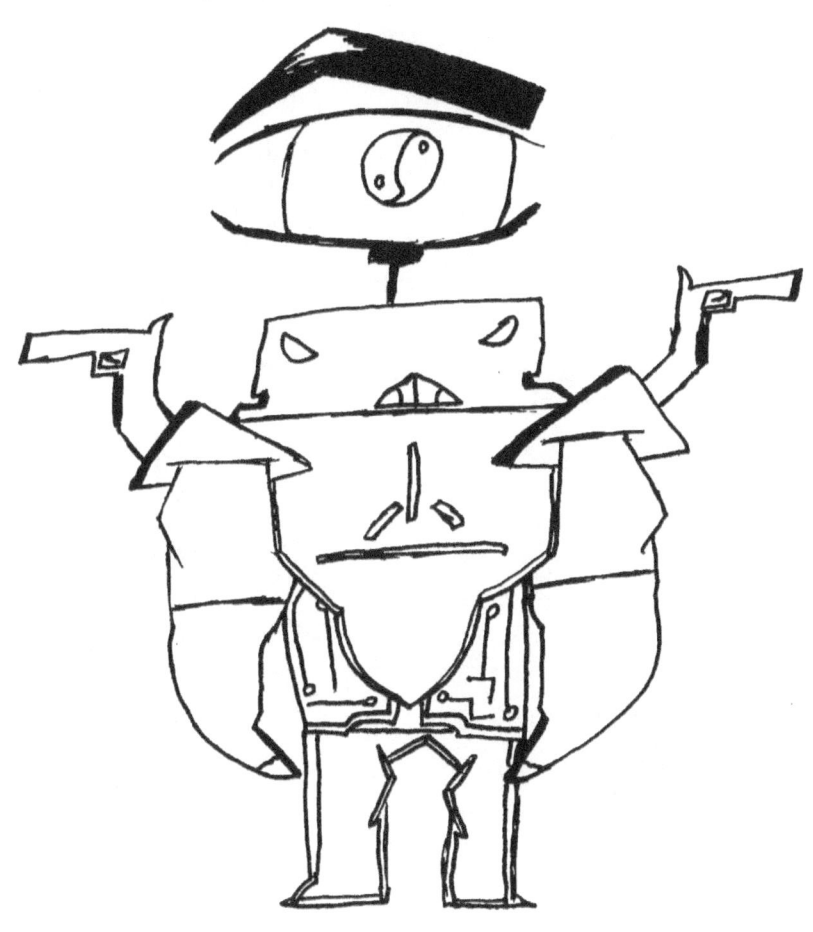

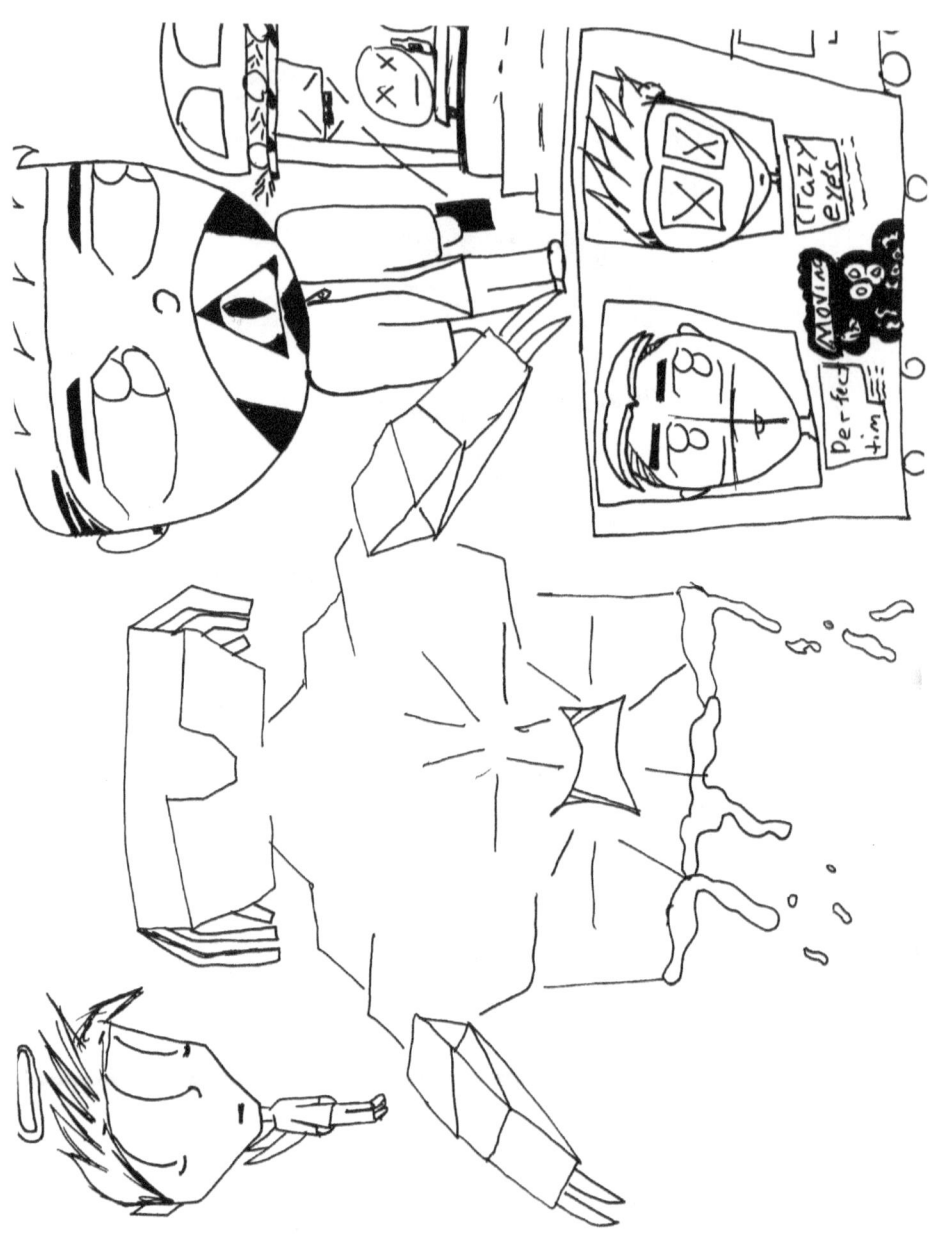

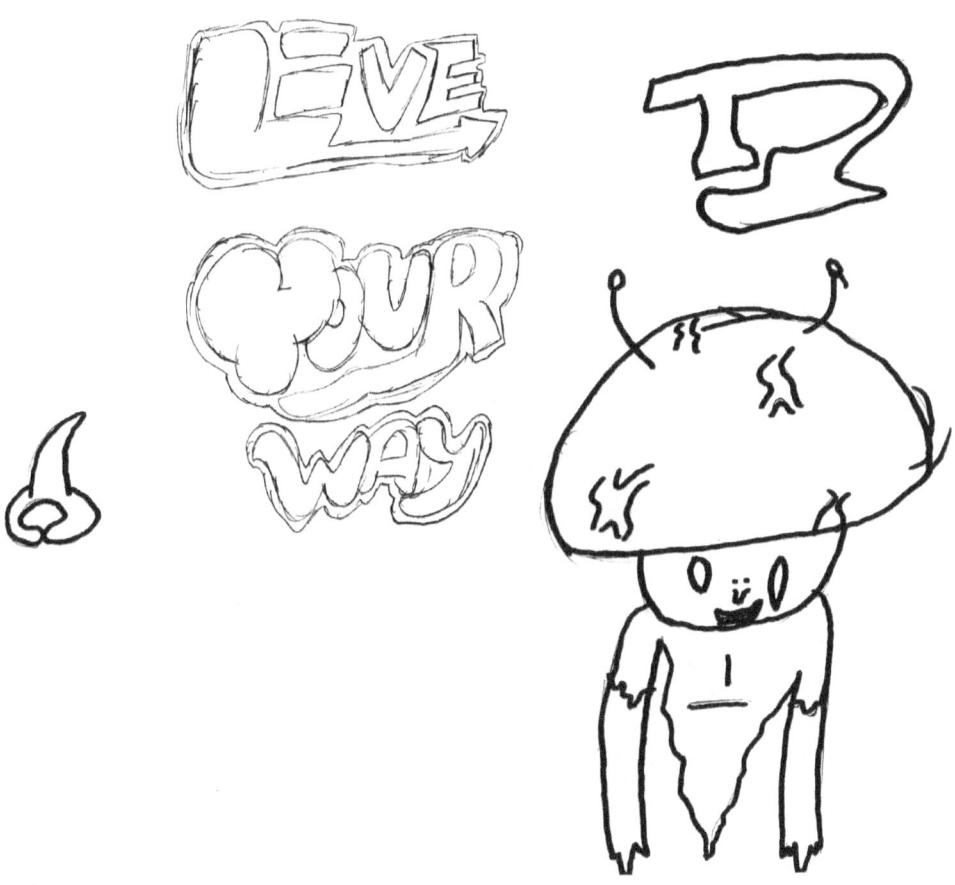

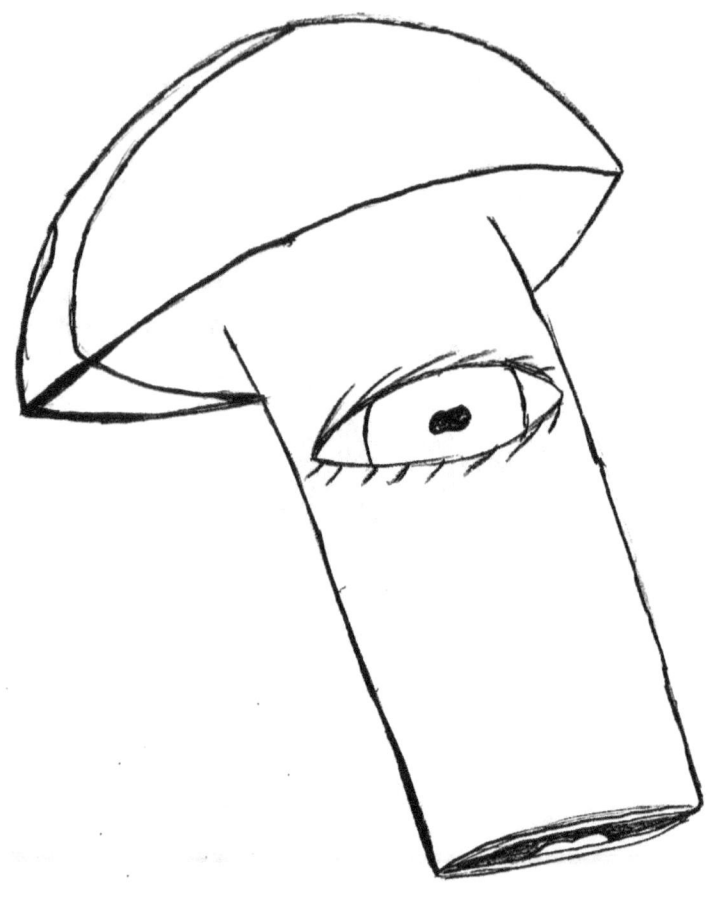

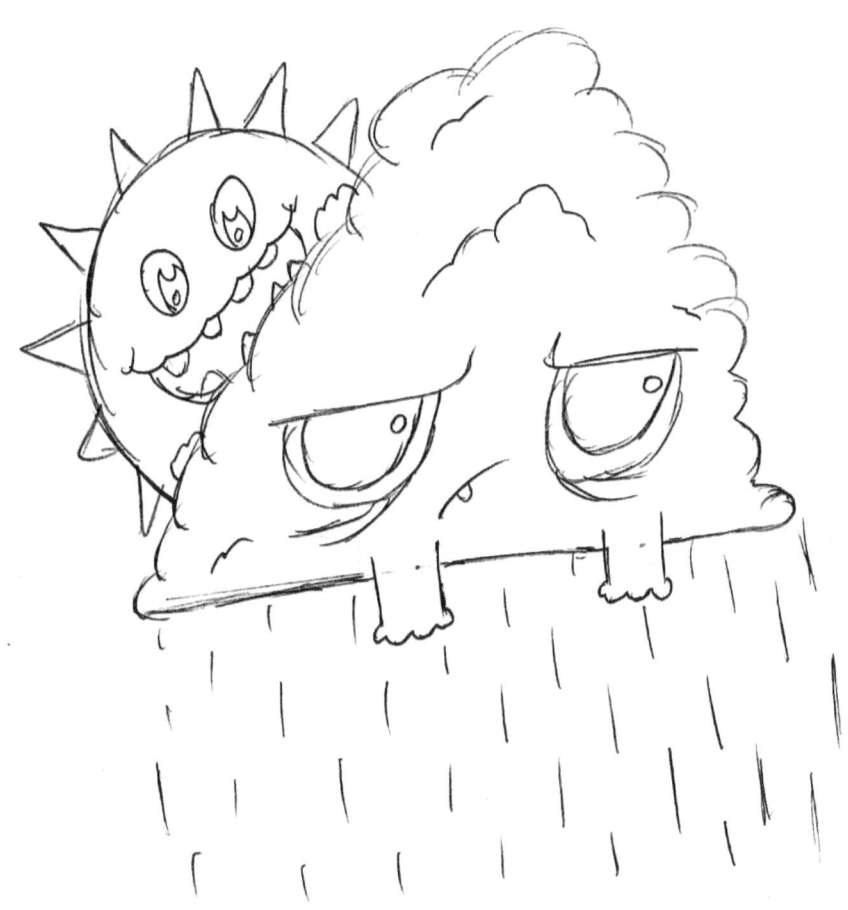

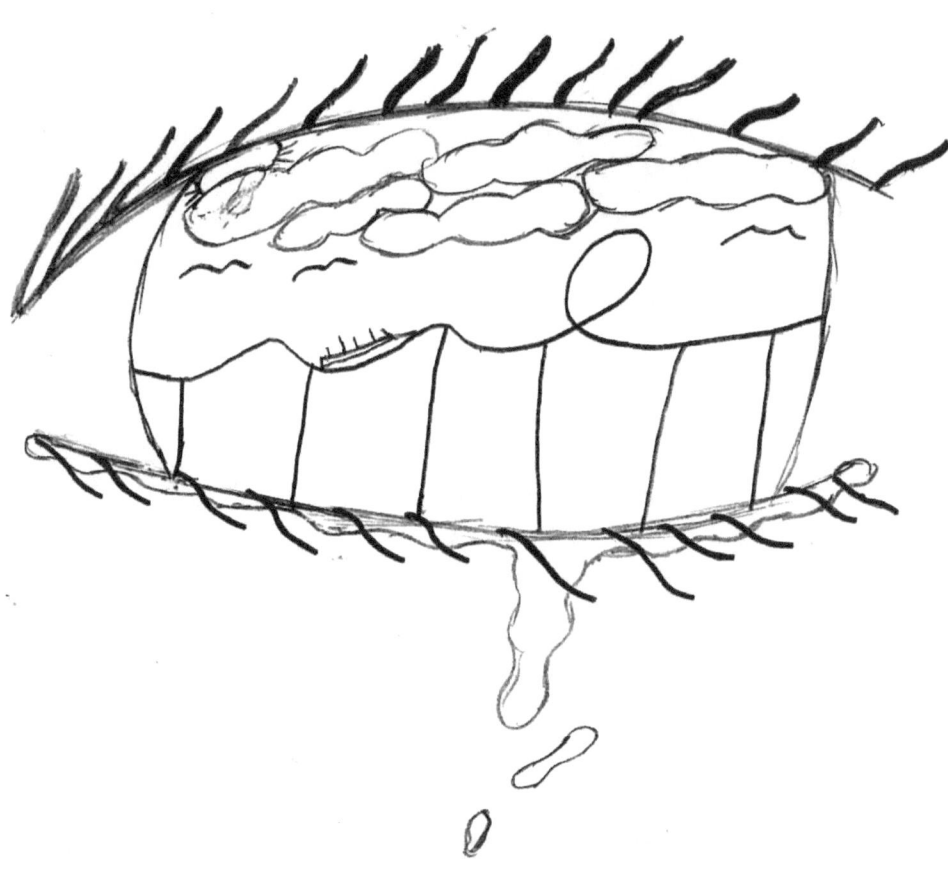

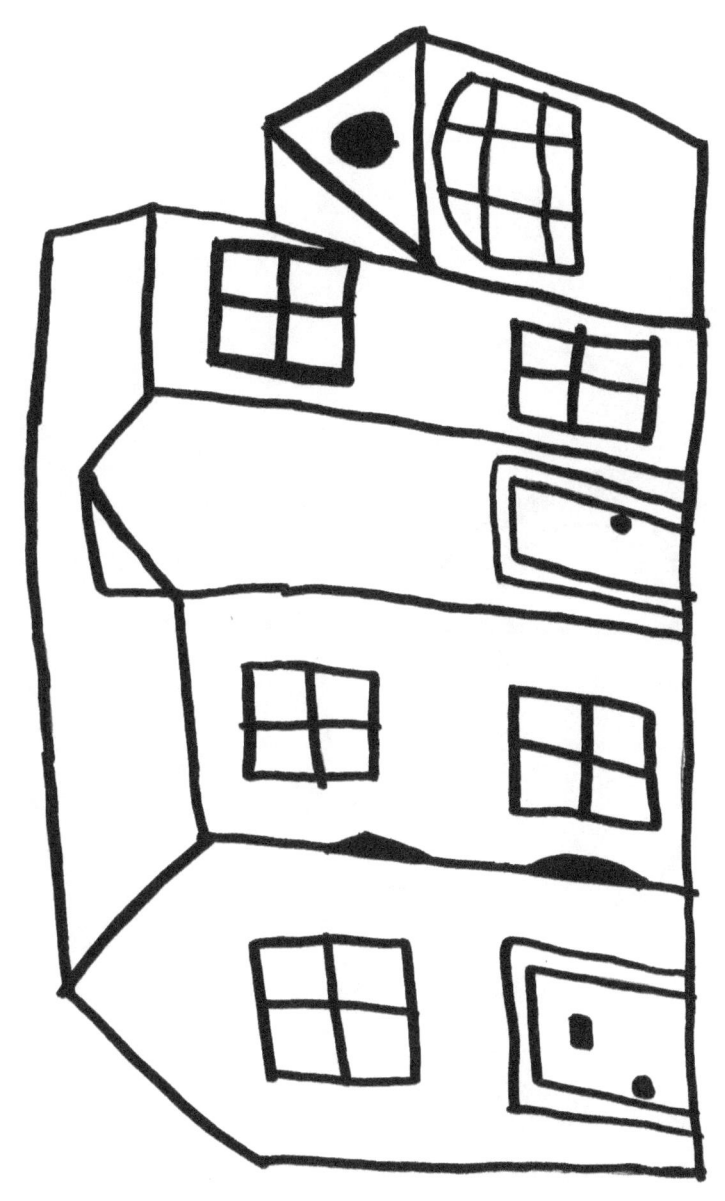

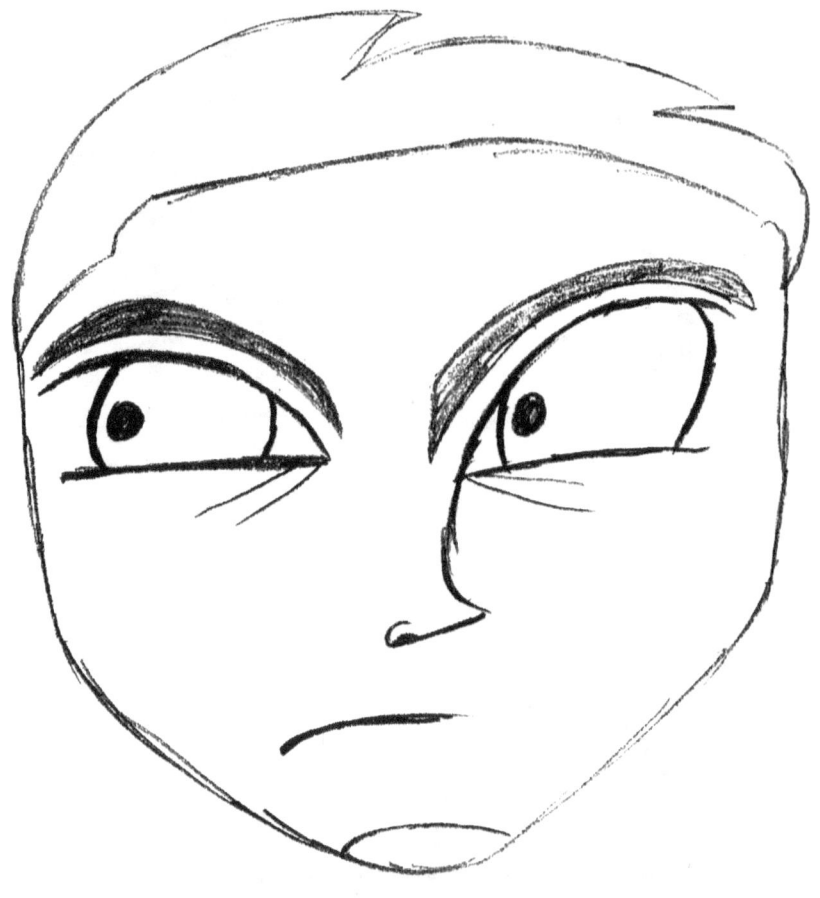

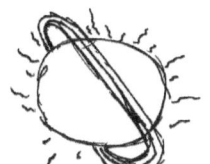

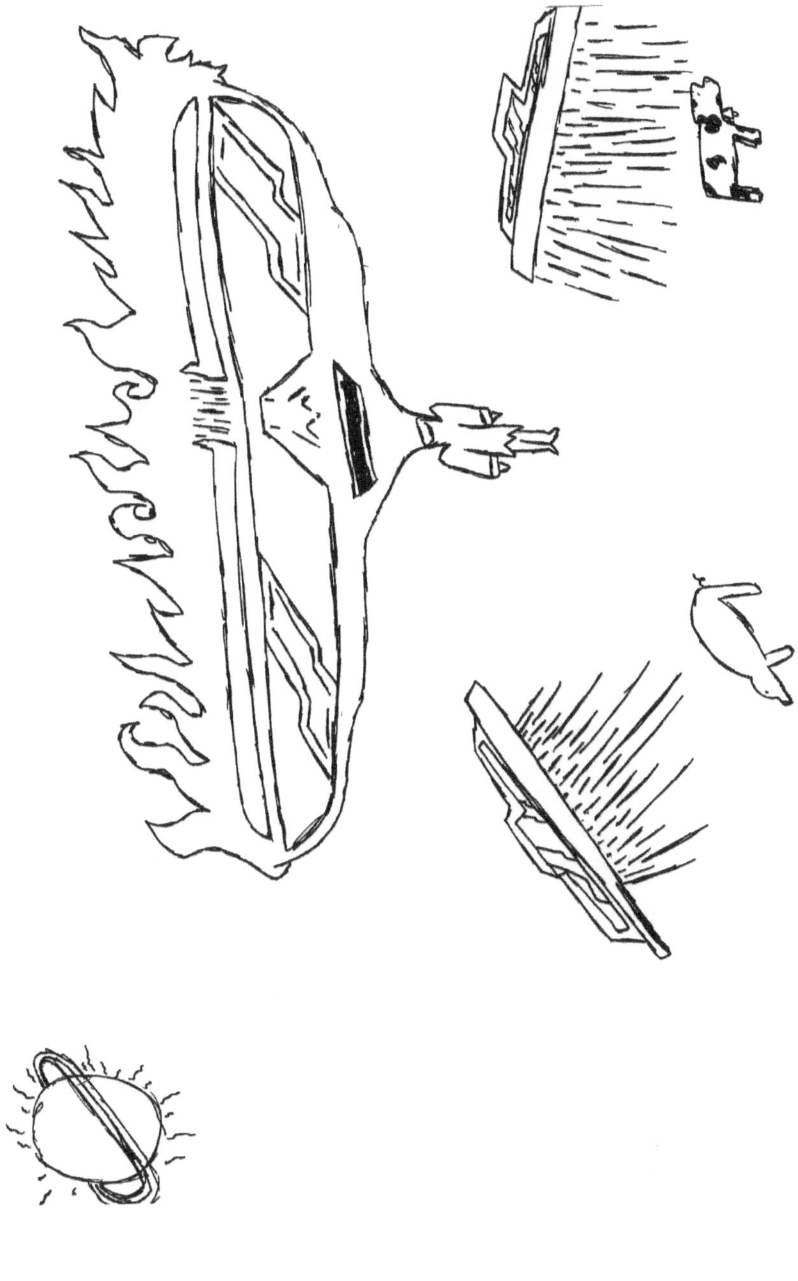

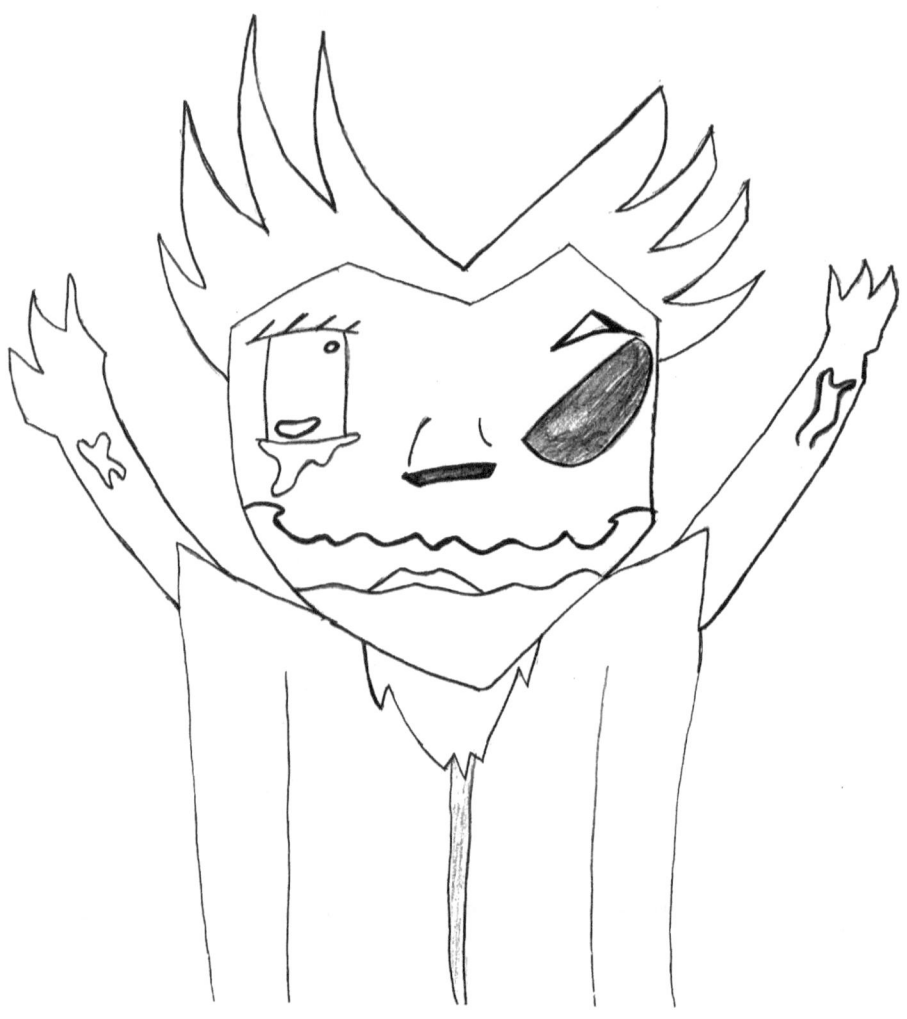

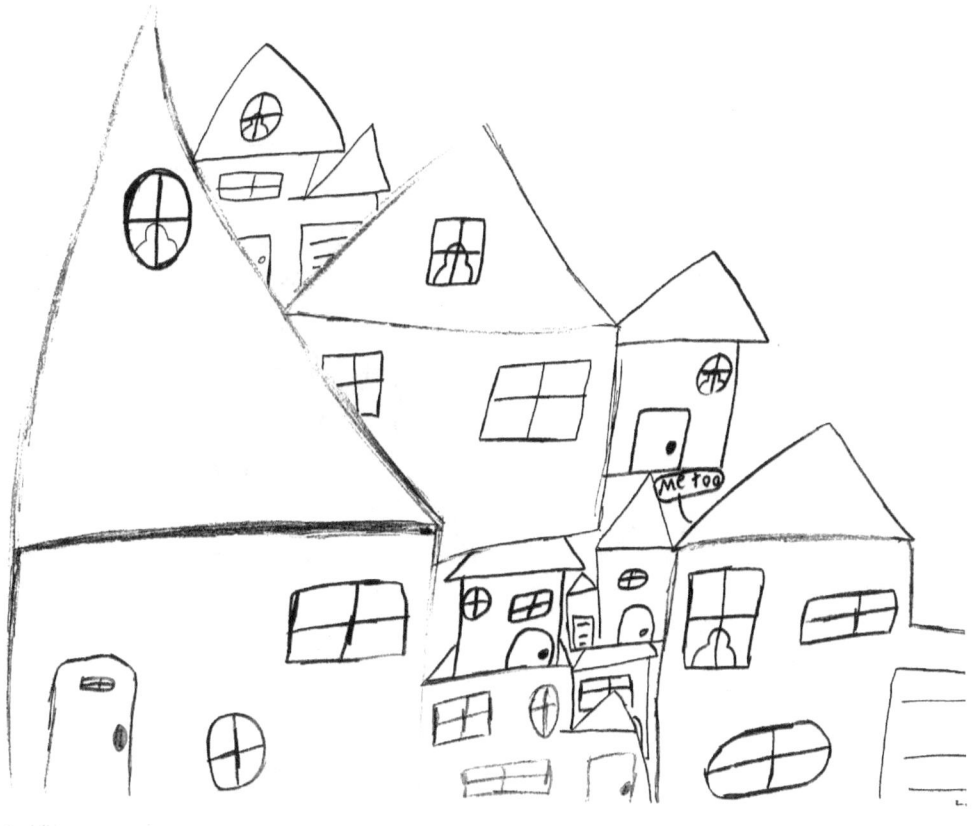

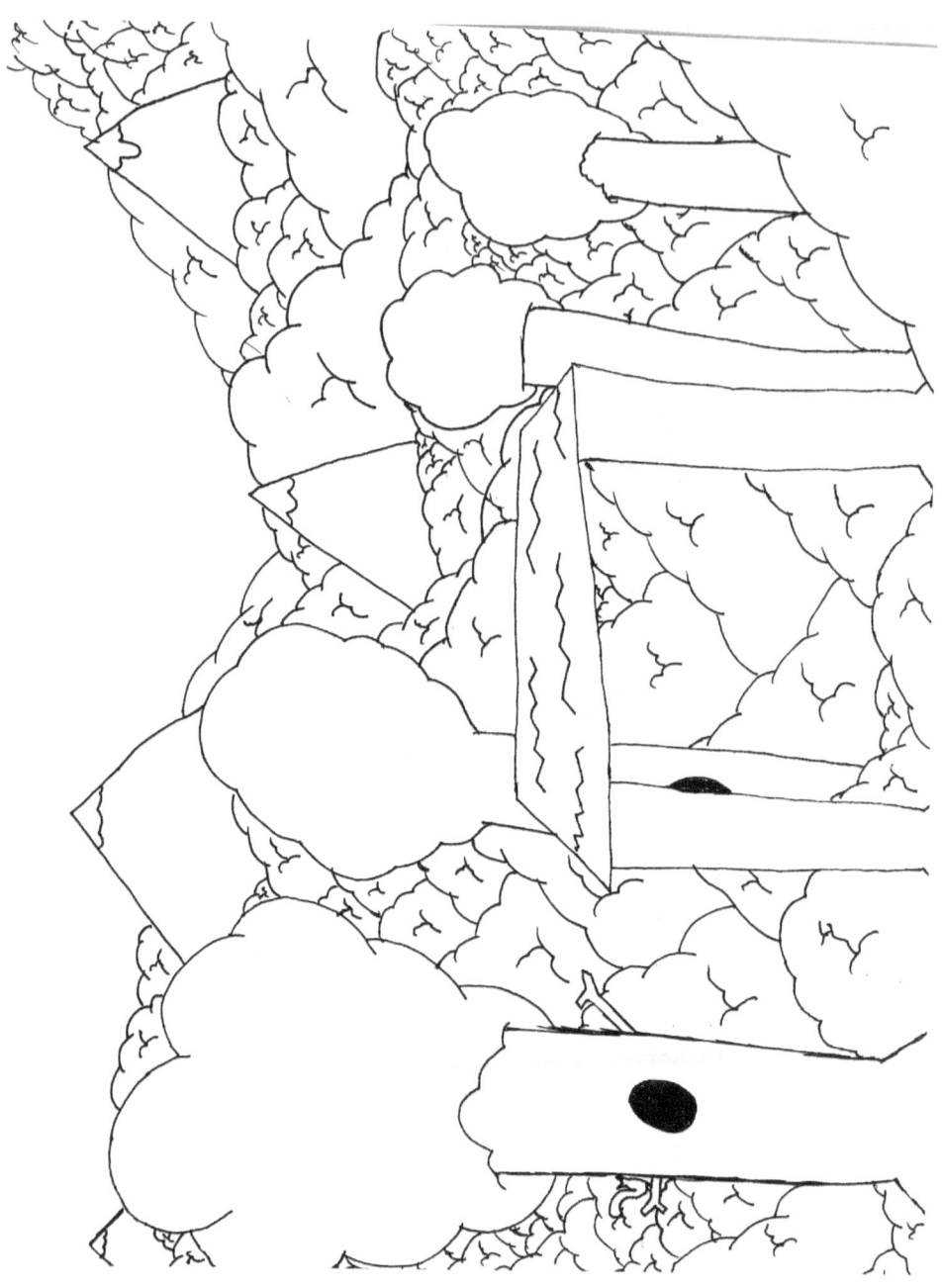

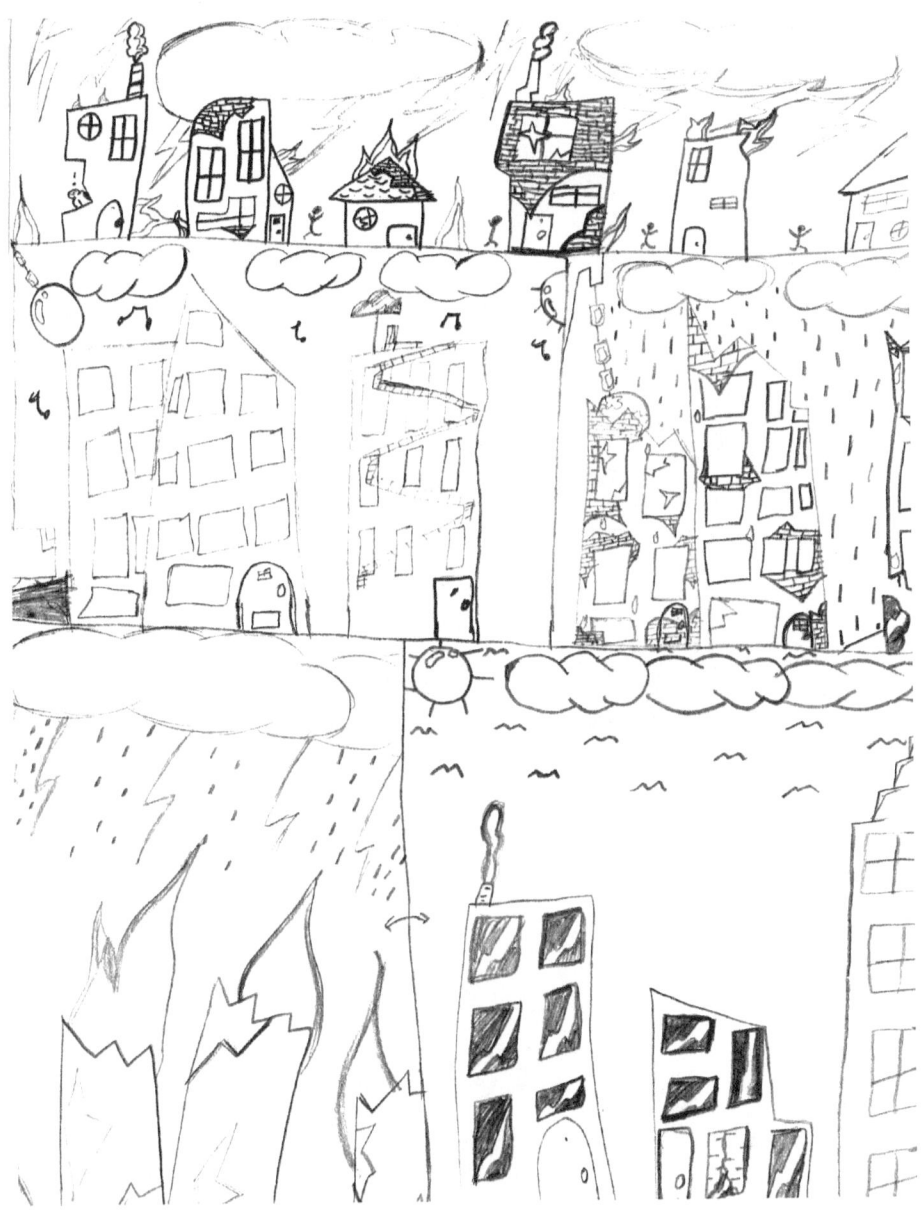

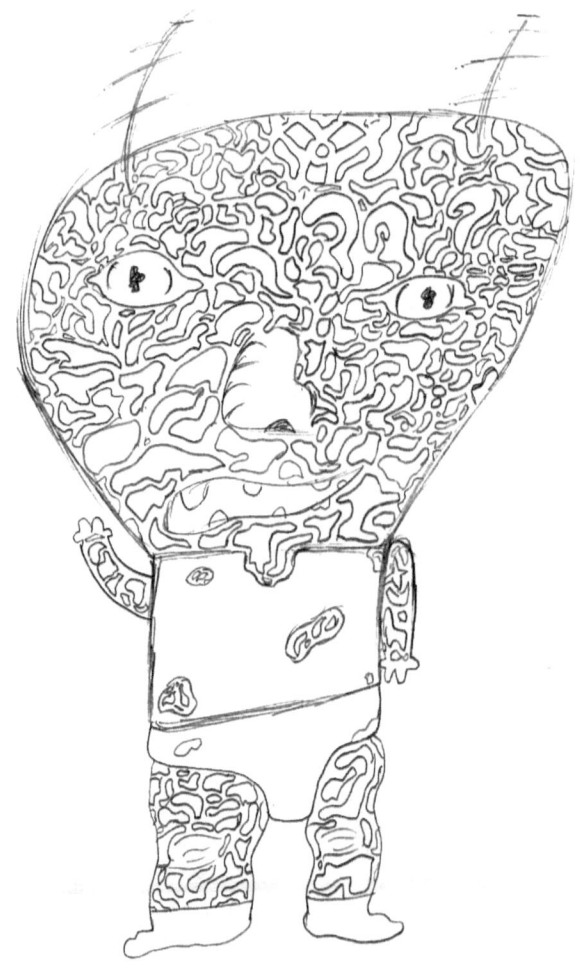

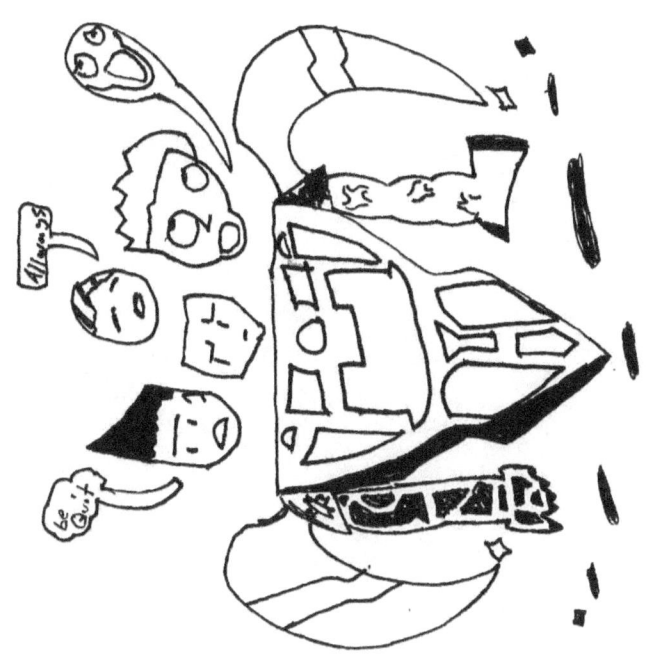
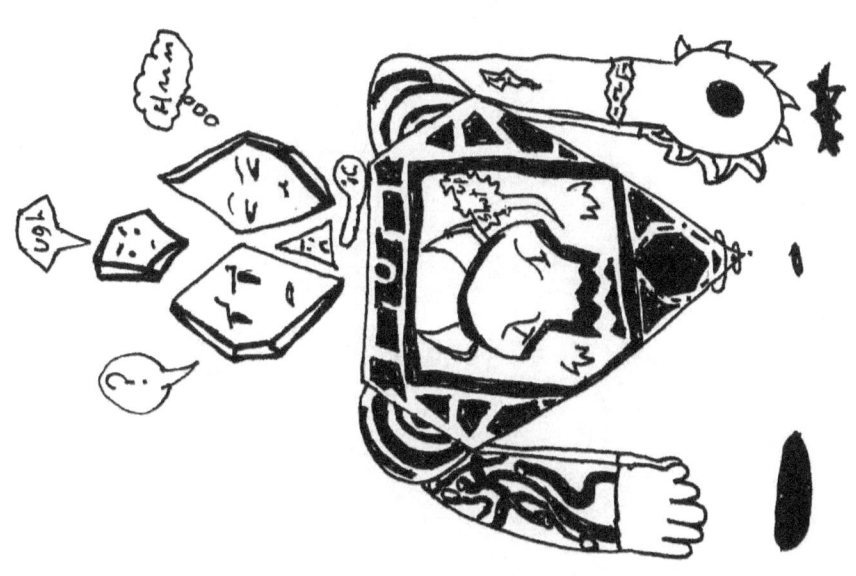

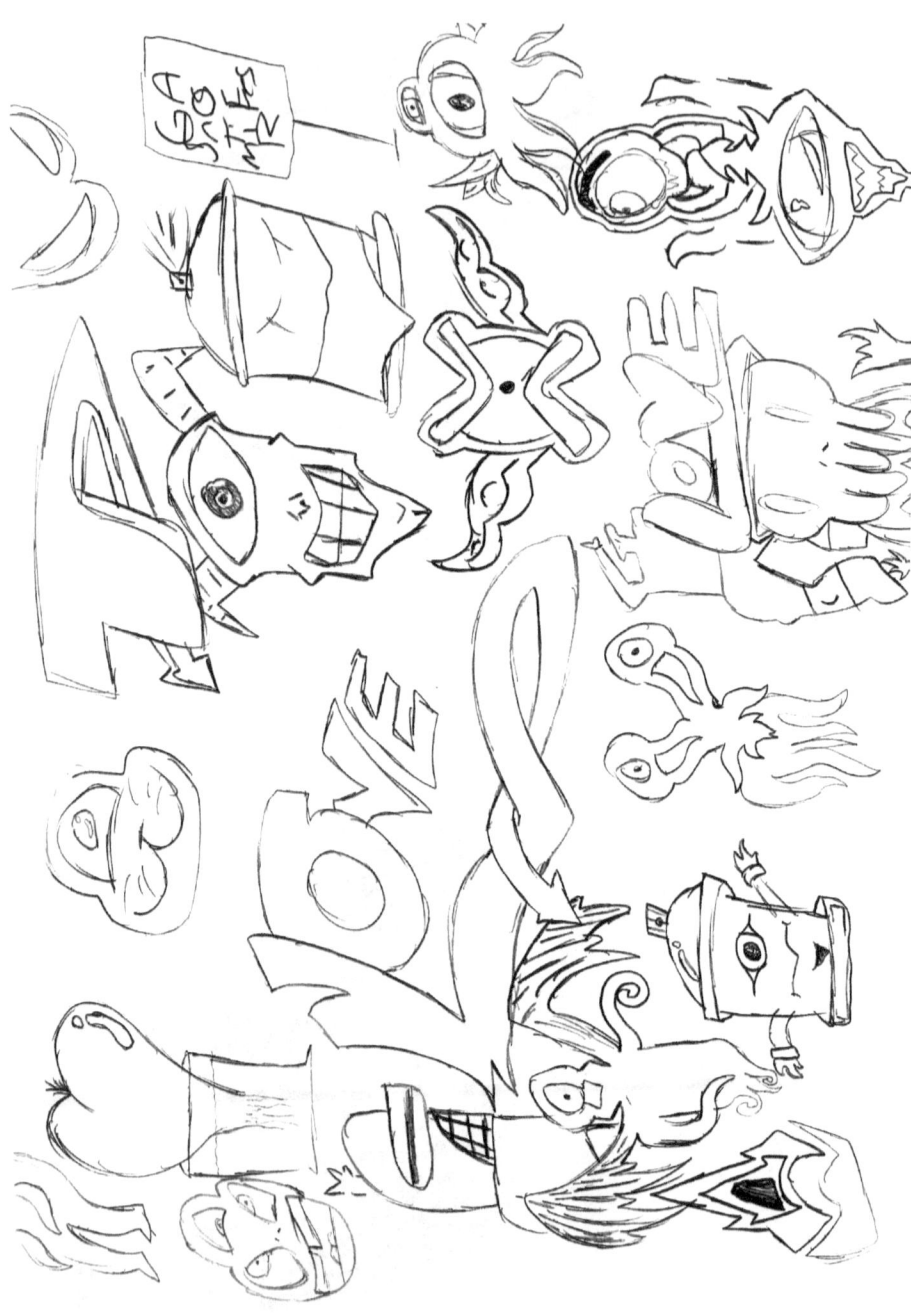

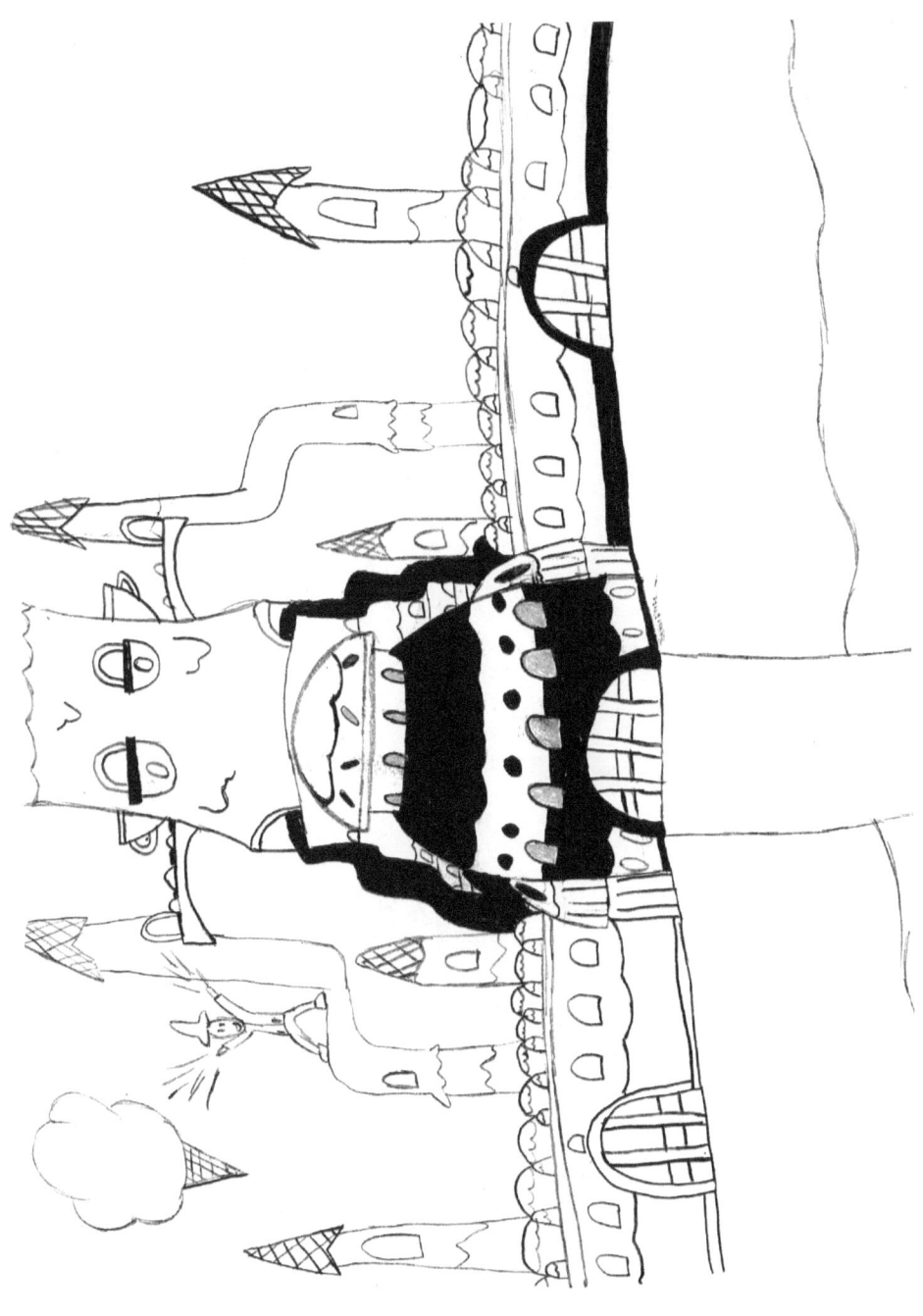

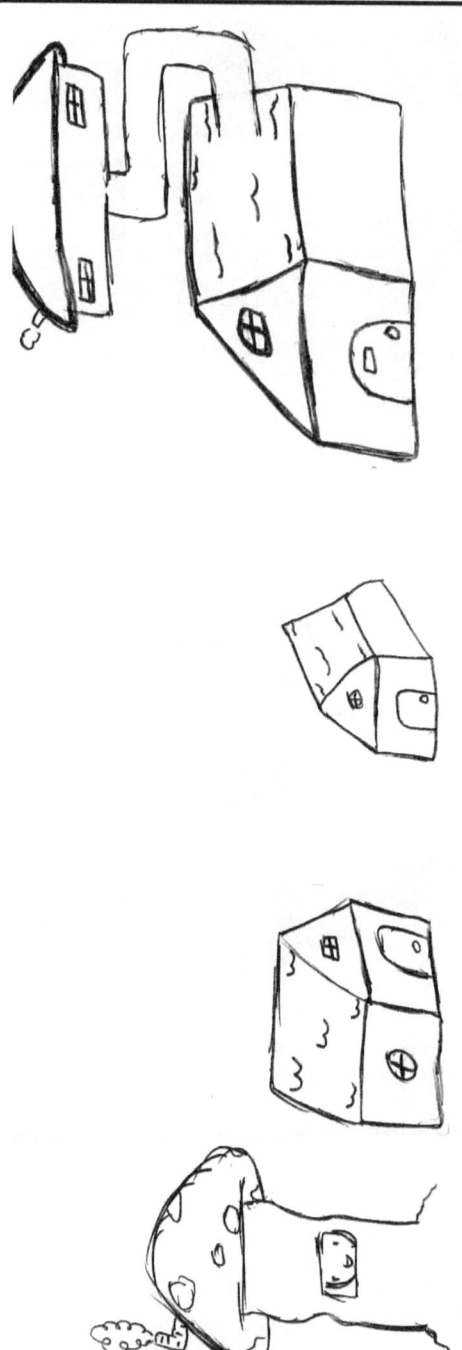

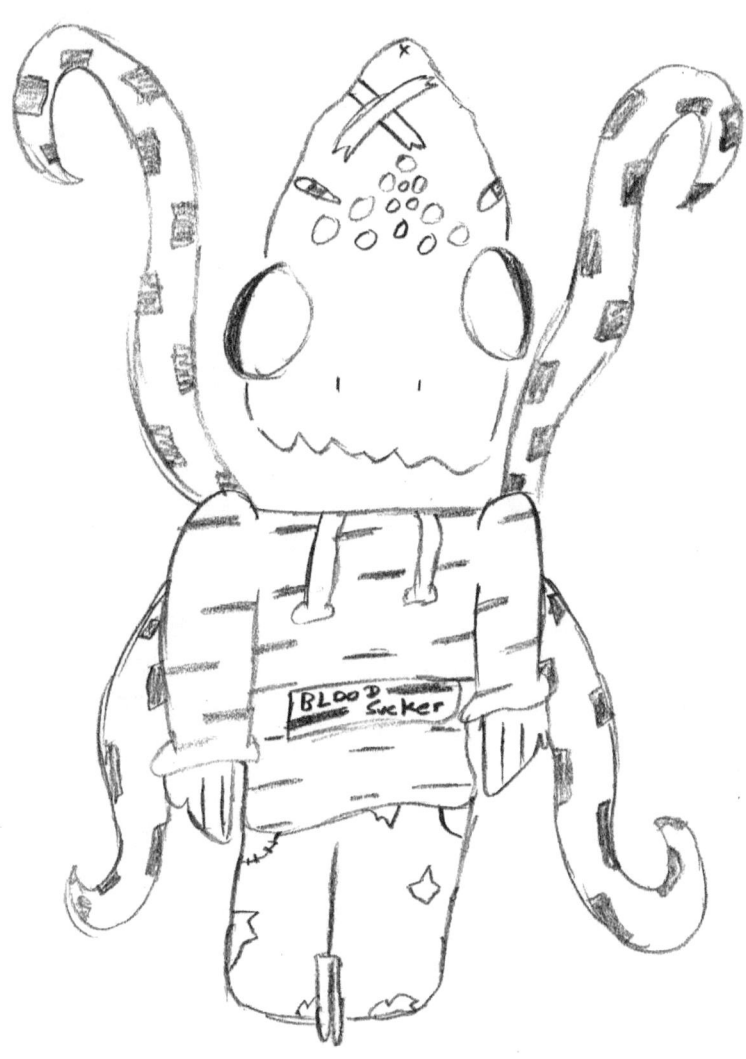

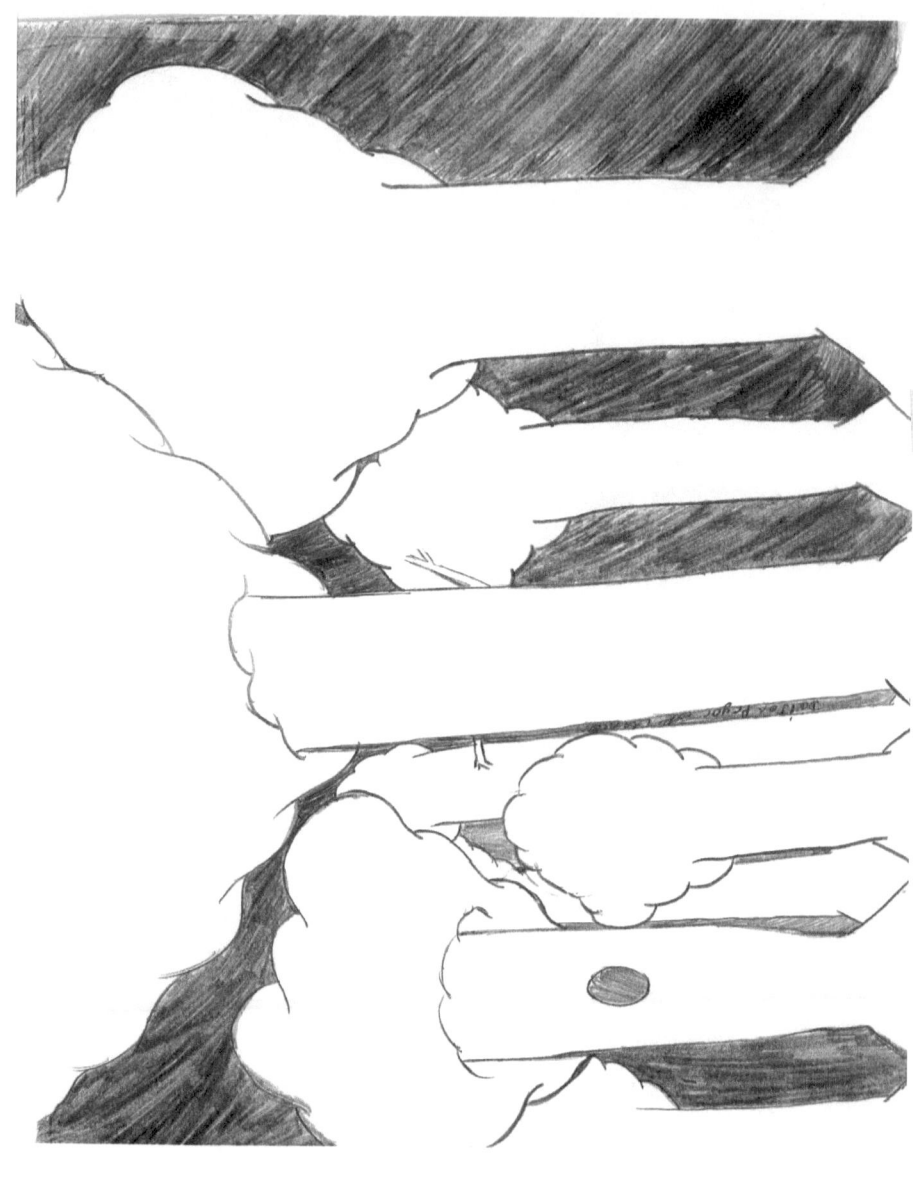

www.ingramcontent.com/pod-product-compliance
Lightning Source LLC
Chambersburg PA
CBHW031540210526
45464CB00003B/1083